LATIN AMERICAN STUDIES
VOLUME 24
Johannes Wilbert, *Series Editor*

Cover design by Alice McGaughey
· Photographs by De Booy, courtesy
Collections of the University Museum, Philadelphia

YUPA FOLKTALES

Johannes Wilbert

Latin American Center
University of California · Los Angeles
1974

Preface

Folklorists and anthropologists engaged in organizing and analyzing collections of narrative materials are all too cognizant of the fact that these tasks require much patience and above all much time. I was fortunate, therefore, to have had the collaboration of several persons to whom I feel deeply indebted: Charlotte Treuenfels for the translations and her help with the proofing, Karin Simoneau for her assistance with the indexing, and Peter T. Furst and Lawrence C. Watson for editorial assistance rendered. Kenneth Ruddle was kind enough to read the completed manuscript and to suggest several improvements. Arnim Truchsess drew the fine artwork.

Charles B. Hitchcock's photograph plate 1, is courtesy of the *Geographical Review* (Vol. 44, 1954), copyrighted by the American Geographical Society of New York. Plates 2–12, 15, and 19 are prints made from photographs by Theodor de Booy, 1915, in the Collections of the University Museum, Philadelphia. Plates 13, 14, and 16–18, are courtesy of Luis T. Laffer, Caracas.

The study was carried out in connection with the Venezuelan Indian Project, sponsored jointly by the Latin American Center of the University of California, Los Angeles, and the Centro Latinoamericano de Venezuela, Caracas. To the La Salle Foundation of Natural Sciences, Caracas, to the Research Institute for the Study of Man, New York, and to all persons and institutions that have aided me in writing this book I express my most sincere feelings of gratitude.

Johannes Wilbert
Eagle Mountain, California
June, 1973

Contents

PREFACE v

INTRODUCTION xi

PART ONE: ETHNOGRAPHY AND NARRATIVE REALITY

The Yupa and the External World 3
    The People of the Mountains 3
    Languages and Subtribes 5
    The Powers of Heaven 5
    The Yupa on This Earth 7
    The Dwarfs Below the Earth 8
    The Europeans from Across the Sea 20
    The Promised Land 23

Manufacturing and Building 27
    Processing the Basic Materials 27
    Houses and Settlements 29

Making a Living 30
    Growing Food 30
    Useful Plants and Food Collecting 32
    Hunting 32
    Fishing 40
    Domestic Animals 41
    Eating, Drinking, and Smoking the Pipe 43

The Society 48
    Family and Kinship 48
    Chiefs and Shamans 48

The Life Cycle 52
    Conception and Pregnancy 52
    Birth and Infancy 52
    Childhood 54
    Puberty and Adolescence 55
    Marriage and Adulthood 56
    Sickness and Death 59

PART TWO: NARRATIVE MATERIAL AND MOTIF CONTENT

The Folktales
    1. The Creation of the First Human Being 75
    2. Day and Night 76
    3. The Flood 78
    4. The Rainbow 78
    5. The Origin of Fire 79
    6. The Land of the Dead 80

7. The Origin of Tubers and Bananas 84
8. In the Land of the Dwarfs 86
9. The Yupa and the Manapsa 90
10. The Origin of the Whites and Their Technology 92
11. The Irapa and the Pariri 95
12. Pareracha—the Red Stone 97
13. Atapoinsha, the Invisible War Hero 97
14. An Attack of the Meteru 98
15. The Great Dying 99
16. The *Chicha* of the Dwarfs 103
17. The Man Who Married His Cousin 103
18. Slander 105
19. The Stingy Daughter-in-law 106
20. Bad Dreams 106
21. Blood Feud 107
22. The Woman Who Fished 109
23. Konochtari, the Centipede 109
24. The Deceiving Mother-in-law 110
25. When There Were But Few Women 111
26. Women Who Want To Be Men 112
27. The Man and the Dog 113
28. Aroka, the Anteater 114
29. Karau, the Lord of the Animals 116
30. The Unsuccessful Hunter 116
31. Yamore, the Deceiver 117
32. Wild Boars and Monkeys 118
33. Amusha, the Deer 118
34. Sanáyamū, the Snake 119
35. Kirikmámare, the Mother of Snakes 120
36. Saroro, the Otter 121
37. Pishicáracha, the Bat 122
38. Piri, the Little Stinging Flies 123
39. The Hummingbird Kuishna 124
40. Wahiku, the Pipe Clay 126
41. The Origin of Maize 127
42. The Origin of Tubers 131
43. Arare, the Tapir 136
44. Karau, the Spirit of the Night 137
45. Karau, the Hunter 138
46. Mashíramū, the Bush Spirit 139
47. Opi, the Spirits of the Night 140

Tale Fragments
48. The House of the Moon 141
49. Chikimo 141
50. Advice for Hunters 142
51. The Tapirs 142
52. Wild Boars 143

53. Snakes 143
54. Trees 143

PART THREE: MOTIF DISTRIBUTION AND INDICES

MOTIF DISTRIBUTION BY MOTIF GROUPS........................... 147
MOTIF DISTRIBUTION BY NARRATIVE 151
THE TOPICAL MOTIF INDEX 154
THE ALPHABETICAL MOTIF INDEX.................................. 165

GLOSSARY 181

BIBLIOGRAPHY.. 187

Introduction

The folktales of the present collection I gathered among the Pariri subtribe of the Yupa Indians. In May 1960 I took an expedition of the La Salle Society of Natural Sciences, Caracas, to the Sierra de Perijá in western Venezuela, where the Yupa Indians live. It was the fourth Yupa expedition of the Society carried out for the specific purpose of collecting further data on the culture and the habitat of this indigenous people (cf. Sociedad de Ciencias Naturales La Salle 1953). Subsequent to this visit, I had the opportunity for additional fieldwork on three different trips to other subtribes of the Yupa (i.e., Irapa, Shaparu, Macoita), and altogether spent three months among these Indians. It was hardly enough time for an in-depth study of the culture of a society, but the collected data combined with the results of a comprehensive study of the Yupa literature provide interesting insights into the life-style of the tribe (Wilbert 1962a).*

In May 1960, while the other members of the aforementioned La Salle expedition concentrated on the ethnobotanical and ethnographical investigations, I became acquainted with two elderly Pariri women who consented to narrate the stories contained herein. The two women were sisters, and with the assistance of the bilingual (Yupa-Spanish) adult son of one of the narrators, it took me two weeks of very intensive work to write down the translations of my interpreter.

The collection of Yupa folktales presented here for the first time in English comprises fifty-four narratives which, except for two or three published by Wavrin (1937), are the only ones in print. I have presented parts of the material in German on two previous occasions, but only as a sample of Yupa mythology appended to an ethnographical report (1962a) or as an uncommentated collection of folktales (1962b).

By casting the texts into their present format and language, I intend, first of all, to make them accessible to a larger audience as well as more manageable for comparative and analytical studies. The summaries and motif inventories at the end of each narrative, and especially the topically and alphabetically arranged apparatus at the end of the book, will greatly contribute to the attainment of this objective. No claim is made to have exhausted the potential motif content of the corpus. The 303 motifs that were identified, however, comprise a useful dictionary of Yupa verbal art.

The motifs are phrased and coded according to Thompson's *Motif-Index of Folk Literature* (1932-36). The obvious advantage of the Topical Motif Index of this volume is that it permits at once inspection of material of similar content. It also identifies the Index key itself. The Alphabetical Motif Index allows the verification of the occurrence of a particular element or motif in Yupa folk literature. Motifs marked with a (+) are extensions of the corresponding Thompson motif which follows in parentheses, facilitating the immediate comparison of any particular pair. Only in one case (narrative 10) did I find it necessary to phrase a new motif and to assign a new motif number.

A second reason for presenting the folktales in context with ethnographical data is to introduce the reader to the milieu, and especially to demonstrate the usefulness of studying the "narrative reality" expressed by the Indians in conjunction with the "ethnographical reality" observed by the anthropologist. Therefore I have systematized the cultural material contained in the narratives and incorporated it into the ethnographical record wherever it appeared opportune to do so.

It is important to point out that by calling the folkloristically derived ethnographical data "narrative reality" I intend to steer clear of the simplistic notion that folklore mirrors culture on a one-to-one correspondence (Simmons 1961:136-140). Instead, I want narrative reality to designate no more and no less than the reality expressed through the folktales. As such it is governed by its own laws of reality. It is certainly partly autobiographical reality (Boas 1916), and it also provides partly a mirror of opposites (Benedict 1935), of wish fulfillment and of behavioral ideals. But all these characteristics do not render the narrative reality unreal or, for that matter, less real than the ethnographical reality. Instead, to look at the narrative reality in a relativistic way permits its acceptance as an important part of the overall cultural reality of a particular society and as the compliment of the ethnographical documentation.

Unfortunately, our knowledge of Yupa culture does not allow full analysis of their ethnography and folktales along the lines of what Dundes (1967:66) calls the "culture reflector" approach. As yet, Yupa anthropology has simply not reached a stage sufficiently advanced to make possible a study approaching the incomparable work done by Boas (1916; 1935), who pioneered this approach, or the work of some of his followers.** Yet the example set forth in this book should bear some evidence at least to the fact that the systematic establishment of the narrative reality of a given corpus of folktales and, hopefully, a subsequent comparison of the same with other such folklore realities is an approach that ought to be encouraged; it produces a kind of insight into a particular culture that is difficult to obtain in any other way. Thus chapters three, four, six and seven of the first part of this book would probably not have been written at all, had it not been for this approach. Of the other chapters of the ethnographical introduction, some have thereby benefitted richly, others only moderately so.

The reader should have no difficulty in determining the source, folkloristic or ethnographical, of a particular piece of information. The data of the narrative reality are always succeeded by the number (in parentheses) of the narrative from which the information was gleaned. Considering the incipient stage of Yupa research, I have refrained from drawing conclusions based on a juxtaposition of the data which, while highly desirable in the future, appears somewhat premature at present.

*The Yupa literature contained in the Venezuelan Indian File in my possession includes the texts of more than 400 sources (cf. O'Leary 1963:36–38). Fuchs (1964:251) has published his ethnographical bibliography of Venezuela with many entries on the Yupa. But it is due to the works by Díaz-Ungría and Castillo (1971) and Ruddle (1970a, 1970b, 1973, 1974) that our knowledge of the tribe has been advanced in recent years.

**Benedict for the Zuni (1935), Ehrlich for the Crow (1937), Reichard for the Coer D'Alène (1947:36–53), Stern for the Klammath (1963). See Simmons (1961) for an African example and for his discussion of the validity of this analytical approach.

I: Ethnography and
Narrative Reality

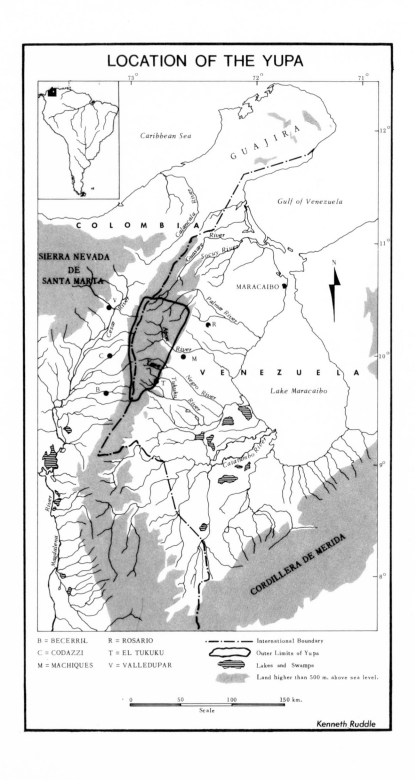

LOCATION OF THE YUPA

Caribbean Sea

GUAJIRA

Gulf of Venezuela

COLOMBIA

SIERRA NEVADA
DE
SANTA MARTA

MARACAIBO

VENEZUELA

Lake Maracaibo

CORDILLERA DE MERIDA

B = BECERRIL   R = ROSARIO

C = CODAZZI   T = EL TUKUKU

M = MACHIQUES   V = VALLEDUPAR

—·—·— International Boundary

   Outer Limits of Yupa

   Lakes and Swamps

   Land higher than 500 m. above sea level.

0   50   100   150 km.

Scale

Kenneth Ruddle

The Yupa and the External World

THE PEOPLE OF THE MOUNTAINS

The ancestors of the present-day Yupa were inhabitants of the lowlands of Venezuela. As a result of the German-Spanish Conquest, in the early sixteenth century, and in later centuries because of the encroachments of Creole ranchers, the Indians were forced to abandon their hunting grounds between Lake Maracaibo and the Sierras and to take refuge in the rugged terrain of the mountains. The highlands afforded the desired security from the depredations of the whites, but at the cost of having to fight the Indians into whose territory they had intruded. Furthermore, the new environment imposed stringent conditions to which the lowland Yupa were not accustomed. Nevertheless, without actually ever adapting their lowland technology completely to the highlands, they developed a new life-style quickly and effectively enough to turn their new home into a viable refuge area beyond the devastating reach of the non-Indian invaders.

For several centuries, then, the Yupa have inhabited the Sierra de Perijá between 9° and 11° N and between 72° 40' and 73° 30' W. The mountain range of Perijá forms the natural border between Venezuela and Colombia. The political border crosses over its highest peak, whence the rivers flow toward the east into Lake Maracaibo and toward the west into the César river, a tributary of the Magdalena. Actually, the Yupa occupy only the Serranía de Valledupar, which forms the northern section of the Sierra de Perijá; the southern section, known as the Serranía de los Motilones, is settled by the Barí Indians.

A characteristic feature of the steep mountains, which rise to 3,630 m at the summit of Manatara, and 3,750 m at Pico Tetarí, are the chasms cut through the rocky walls by the turbulent cascades of countless tropical rainy seasons. Rain varies altitudinally, regionally, and seasonally but falls throughout the year, so that the rivers are never completely dry even in summer.

The deep river valleys of the Sierra function as effective political boundaries between the Yupa subtribes. Each group is also socioeconomically limited to its own territory by three different thermal zones. Scattered observations have shown that the highest

3

elevations, the *páramos* (3,500 m) and the cold zone (2,000–3,500 m), are marked by cold nights (*páramos* 9° C–3° C, cold zone 16° C–10° C) and by desiccated, virtually barren spurs and ridges. In a second, temperate zone (800–2,000 m), dense forests reach to considerable heights, and for part of each day and night, fog envelops everything in a blanket of heavy moisture, with temperature ranges between 23° C and 17° C. The higher the forest the cooler the temperature; the vegetation soon becomes insufficient to sustain higher life forms. The Indians prefer to settle at lower altitudes, either within the hot zone (0–800 m), with temperatures between 28° C and 24° C, or in temperate areas up to 1,400 m above sea level. Here horticulture is possible and a variety of crops may be grown (Gusinde 1956*a;* Hitchcock 1954; Ruddle, 1970*a*, 1973).

Just which tribes were displaced by the Yupa is not possible to ascertain at the present time. Among them might have been the Chibchan-speaking Arahuakos (Kogi, Ica, Sanka) whose descendants today inhabit the Sierra Nevada de Santa Marta west of Perijá entirely on Colombian soil, and/or the Chibchan-speaking Bari who now reside in areas south of Yupa territory.

In their folk literature the Yupa preserve remote echoes of these historic hostilities. One narrative (14) mentions a raiding party of so-called Meteru Indians who attack a Yupa settlement. But an outright war of expansion against the Meteru is described in another story (13), which begins by relating that "one day when the Yupa sought to move into a new land, they found it occupied by the powerful tribe of the Meteru." They pushed them down the mountains into the swamps, "down where the Negro flows into the Santa Ana." This was dangerous territory inasmuch as it was more accessible to the Conquistadores. But, so concludes the story, "Since this time the Yupa have lived in the mountains of Perijá, and the Barí, the few descendants of the Meteru, live in the part further south of the Sierra."

My informants identified the Meteru with the Barí, with whom the Yupa were still at war in 1960 when some Capuchin missionaries and I, among others, succeeded in contacting the Barí peacefully. The Manapsa Indians, also mentioned in Yupa oral literature, may be de Booy's (1918*a*:498, 1918*b*:212) Arahuacos. According to one narrative (9), sporadic contact through intertribal marriages may have occurred between the Yupa and the Manapsa, in the course of which considerable culture borrowing must have taken place. But eventually the Manapsa were defeated by the Yupa, and following Yupa history: "The Yupa were thus later able to settle on the land where their old neighbors, the Manapsa, had formerly lived" (9).

LANGUAGES AND SUBTRIBES

Yupan is of Cariban stock. Internal divergence of its component languages and dialects is sufficient to impede mutual intelligibility between maximally divergent tongues of the family; for example, Irapan and Japrerian.

Fierce hostility among the subtribes has contributed to isolation and resulting linguistic separation. Apart from territoriality, one of the major factors contributing to conflict has been the kidnapping of women and children, carried out for centuries on an intertribal as well as intratribal basis. Recorded instances go back as far as 1769 and 1744 (Archivo Nacional de Colombia, t. 20, f. 814).

Following Ruddle's (1971:22) demographic data, the Yupa subtribes on the Venezuelan side of the Sierra break down as follows: Irapa 588, Japreria 47, Macoita 250, Pariri 101, Rionegrino 120, Shaparu 50, Viakshi 9, Wasama 70, Tukuku Mission Village (minus Irapa) 149, Mission School Children 100; subtotal Yupa 1,484. The Yupa on the Colombian side of the Sierra are known as Yuco. Their subgroups include the following: Iroka 370, Las Candelas 15, Manaure 35, Maracá 120, San Genaro 10, Sokomba 30, Susa 100, Yowa 12; subtotal Yuco 692. According to these most recent figures the entire Yupa population comprises 2,176 individuals.

THE POWERS OF HEAVEN

The Yupa conceive of the earth as a flat disk (Wilbert 1959: 129). Moving around it originally were two suns, one rising when the other went down (2). The two suns were brothers and they illuminated this earth during an eternal day.

Kopecho, the mythical Frog-Woman, changed this state of affairs. Sometime before she was transformed into a frog, Kopecho decided to invite one of the suns to a festival, in the course of

5

which she lured him into a pit of glowing embers. Although the sun, accustomed to heat, survived the ordeal, he turned white, and lost some of his heat and brilliance. He became the moon, but before returning to his place in the sky, tossed Kopecho into the water where she was transformed into Frog-Woman. She is now the judge who tests the souls of dead Yupa on their way to the Otherworld.* Sun and Moon still continue to take their turns illuminating the earth, thereby causing day and night, that is, marking time.

Although brothers, Sun and Moon could never get along with each other (2). Each month Sun orders his allies, the stars, to fall across Moon and castigate him for having once refused a star one of his many daughters. "The moon stoops down then and gets very small" (2).

Sun rules over the stars, and the Jaguar People appear to be his allies. But Sun has no family of his own. He is gluttonous and greedy, and devours people whenever he can get his hands on them (42). Judging from an episode in the same narrative (42), Sun, in preparing a captured man for a cannibalistic feast, drugged the victim with a large quantity of tobacco juice, a custom reminiscent of some Mesoamerican sacrificial practices.

Moon has many daughters but only one son. However, neither Moon's children nor his wife can be seen because they always stay at home. There is a cave up in the skies which Moon's daughters occupy during menstruation (42).

The disposition of Moon and his kin toward man is benevolent. There is the myth according to which a hunter was rescued and protected by Moon's son and by Moon himself. The hunter was given one of Moon's daughters and, before permitting him to return to earth, Moon presented him, and through him, mankind, the handsome gift of several food crops (42).

The Milky Way is the path of Sun and Moon (2). The Rainbow is a man who appears to be fond of Yupa women. He abducts them, much to the detriment of the unfortunate victims (4).

Somewhere up in heaven there also lives a supernatural being who is the creator of man. He has a wife who helped him carry out his plans of creation. Both creator and his consort act in a benevolent and just way toward mankind (1).

*See The Land of the Dead (6).

THE YUPA ON THIS EARTH

We learn of the creator being in Yupa folk literature in a tale in which he roams the earth in search of a suitable tree whose timber might serve as raw material for the creation of man (1). The interpreter chose to call this personage "dios" and explained that the tree finally selected was a *sangrito* (*Vismia* sp.). The creator carved two human children, a boy and a girl, from this wood. He placed them in a wooden box and commanded Woodpecker to hatch them. According to myth, then, plants and animals in general antedate man on earth. The only exceptions, my informant explained, are the plants and animals that were once human beings and that became transformed.

The shaping of the first people and making them come to life were the tasks, respectively, of the creator and Woodpecker. Bringing up the small children, however, was left to a female companion of the creator. She is introduced (1) just as casually as was "god" himself; as might be expected, this woman takes care of the children until puberty. All mankind ultimately traces its origin to this primordial parental pair.

Additional information describes the creator as a transcendental being who is nevertheless sufficiently concerned about mankind to intervene on various critical occasions to establish rules of conduct and to preserve man from ill-fortune.

The first intervention comes about some time after the creation of the primordial human couple. By this time man had reproduced to the extent that "there was a sufficient number of people upon earth" (1). The creator descended to mingle with humankind, to reveal the genesis of man, to prohibit sibling marriage, and, finally—rather typical for departing gods—to establish a commemorative feast promising life after death for all Yupa. We learn on a later occasion (15) how critical is the observation of the incest taboo for the welfare of mankind and how catastrophic the results of transgression.

Since its origin, mankind has passed through several crises which severely reduced its numbers. The first was a universal flood "from which only twenty pairs of human beings and a few animals were able to save themselves on top of a high mountain" (3). It was through the combined efforts of Woodpecker, Tapir, Crab, Cayman, Turtle, Armadillo, and other animals, that a mud wall surrounding the water was destroyed and the flood drained off. The presence among these helpful animals of Woodpecker, who assisted in the original creation of man, comes as no surprise. The cayman, who made the decisive contribution toward his salvation, turned out to be a shaman (3).

A shaman is also called upon to save mankind from another cataclysm, caused by an epidemic of catarrh (15). The story may well have a historical basis, referring to a time when the Yupa first encountered the white man, and through him, the common cold. We know only too well the tragic truth of the narrator's words: "On the way to the new tribal grounds the great dying of the Yupa began. First the children died, then the women, then the men. All of them died, for the *tuano* [shaman] had no remedy to fight this sickness." Eventually, only the shaman and his wife survived, and it is from them that all modern Yupa are said to be descended.

A third crisis occurred when the descendants of this surviving shaman pair disobeyed the incest taboo, which had only temporarily been suspended out of necessity, for lack of people on earth (15). Again torrential rains flooded the earth, causing famine to which many Yupa succumbed. The sun stood still in the zenith, resuming its normal course only after the shaman on a celestial journey succeeded in placating the life-giving star.

THE DWARFS BELOW THE EARTH

Below the plane of this earth, according to Pariri cosmology, there exists an Underworld inhabited by a race of dwarfs—the Pïpïntu. The Indians claim to have obtained their knowledge of this place through the eyewitness account of a man who, trapped in a funerary cave, managed to escape by way of the entrance to this Underworld.

As explained in the narrative (8), the natural environment of the Land of the Dwarfs does not differ markedly from the Yupa habitat on earth. More noteworthy are the somatological peculiarities of the Underworld dwarfs, and the tale focuses heavily on them. In addition, we are also offered an etiological explanation to account for the presence of pygmoid individuals among the Yupa. At this point some brief cultural-historical and comparative remarks are in order to place the biological, ethnographic, and folkloric significance of this tale in proper perspective.

The Pariri family with which I camped in May, 1960, was

polygynous, and one of the wives was pygmoid in stature. She was a very quiet person, who performed her domestic duties with a permanent smile of submissiveness. One evening, after I had spent the day collecting data on the *tomaira* (priest) and his *homáikï* (ritual songs), this little woman came to tell me that "her people," high up in the mountains, knew the "real" *homáikï*. Even she knew so many, she said, that it took from one moon to the next to sing them all. Unfortunately, I never had an opportunity to verify either of these claims, but thereafter, on the several occasions when I lived among the Yupa, I watched for anything that might provide a clue to possible cultural differences between the pygmoid Yupa and the taller majority.

To be sure, I did note differences (cf.Laffer 1959). But they are few, and on closer examination have so far proved inadequate to support the hypothesis of an essential difference between the culture of the pygmoids and the culture of the Yupa. There also appear to be some behavior patterns that set the small-sized Yupa apart from their tall relatives. But these differences hardly constitute complexes pointing to different cultural roots.

We know of the existence of pygmoid individuals among several South American tribes, especially in the northwest. We also know that they have several culture traits and behavior patterns that are peculiar to them and that set them apart from the taller Indians among whom they live. Finally, we know that these differences are shared, at least among the Yupa, by all the sporadically distributed pygmoids. This sharing means that the differences between Yupa of "normal" stature and so-called pygmoids cannot easily be explained by the geographical barriers to diffusion so characteristic of the Yupa habitat, barriers that have resulted in marked differences in language and other traits within the Yupa culture area. It seems equally impossible to explain the differences as adaptive variations in response to ecological conditions, because the pygmoids appear to have shared the same habitat with other Yupa ever since the latter migrated into the Sierra. For the present, and largely for lack of better field material, I prefer to explain the peculiar personal habits of the Yupa pygmoids in terms of response of a subordinate minority group to a superordinate master group. Culture-trait differences may represent cultural lags among the marginal pygmoid minority, which is excluded from participating fully in the processes of cultural development triggered by events from outside. I would hope, however, that ethnologists will be on the alert for any evidence pointing to some other explanation.

One of the more obvious cultural differences between the pygmoids and the Yupa is the technology of fire making. The method that the Master of Fire introduces in one narrative (5), is not, in fact, that commonly employed by the Yupa. The Yupa produce fire by friction, that is, by means of the rotating fire drill. The pygmoids, in contrast, employ two flints, *wéhra-támï* (Cariban) and thus make fire by the percussion technique. According to Yupa tradition, the second method is the original one, and, judging from the distribution of the percussion method of fire making throughout South America, it is in fact likely to be the older of the two. It has been recorded primarily among Paleo/Meso-Indian tribes of the subcontinent, although it is also referred to in the oral literature of the Cariban Taurepan (Koch-Grünberg 1917–1928; 3:47–48), as well as in that of an unidentified Guyana Carib tribe (Roth 1915:192). Our present evidence indicates, however, that the percussion method of fire making has generally not been reported from Cariban tribes.

Another rather obvious difference is loom weaving. It is expertly done by pygmoid women (Bolinder 1925:218), but only occasionally and less expertly by other Yupa women.

A third difference was observed to exist with respect to the prevailing house forms. The majority of the Yupa live in rectangular, saddle-roofed, pole houses; more recently some have also adopted adobe construction. But the pygmoid Yupa live in windbreaks, with the screen either touching the ground directly or resting on a low stone wall. They are carefully constructed and, although much smaller in size, resemble the more permanent windbreak house type of the Yanoama.

The pygmoid Yupa are also the best potters, and the men make excellent composite clay pipes, which in itself is atypical for Cariban tribes. The pygmoids also enjoy the reputation of being good brewers of beer. They make their beer from maize rather than from yuca, as is customary among the Carib.

These differences are insufficient to establish a cultural plurality among the Yupa along the lines of ethnic differentiation. We place them on record simply because they do exist at present, as well as to have them available for future reference, should new field data favor an interpretation of differences in terms of survivals from a distinct pygmoid culture type (Laffer 1959).

Scattered throughout my field notes are references to the behavior and conduct of the pygmoid Yupa by which they are distinguished from the rest of the tribe. One cannot fail to sense an air of distinction about them; they bear themselves in a restrained, self-confident, and dignified manner (Laffer 1959:4). This behavior, of course, is the opposite of what one would expect from a minority group held in almost complete servitude by its masters. Whatever freedom and independence of action the pygmoids do enjoy must be in direct proportion to the respect they are able to demand as proud, dexterous, and diligent people.

For centuries the pygmoid Yupa must have suffered all the humiliations and persecutions that could be dealt out by a majority group to a weaker minority population. Their stoical, impassive expression may be a mask of resignation which they have learned to wear in the interest of self-preservation and survival. Theirs was and continues to be the lot of the serf.

Except as outlined below, I observed that pygmoid women kept themselves at the disposal of their masters. Pygmoid men worked almost daily for the Yupa family in whose proximity they lived and whose protection they enjoyed.

I was told they expected no compensation for their labor and usually managed to supply themselves with sufficient food. Certainly, never would one see them beg. However hungry they might become, they will wait until the master's family has eaten. The modesty and unpretentiousness of the pygmoid Yupa is nothing short of heroic. I have seen their women cook the day's food for a master's family, patiently watch them eat in the evening, and then steal away into a corner of the house with the one handful of yuca that was their daily ration.

Not only are the pygmoids required to work hard for the taller Yupa overlords, but the latter frequently amuse themselves by deliberately seeking to complicate the tasks they give their serfs. This human drama is illustrated in the tale *The Chicha of the Dwarfs* (16). A much ridiculed pygmoid is ordered to prepare a trough full of the best *chicha* for a drinking bout his master was planning. In order to amuse themselves at his expense, the master and his friends placed the trough too high for the pygmoid brewer, who had to use a stepladder to pour the many gourds full of water into the trough, and to reach into it to stir the maize mash. When the brew was ready and the bout began, they removed the stepladder and then graciously invited their serf to join them by savoring the drops that ran down the trough. But the pygmoid, pretending to have no desire to drink *chicha,* picked up his fishing tackle and was granted permission to leave. This not only spared him further humiliation, but enabled him to escape from a certain physical danger. Usually the pygmoid brewers are expected to run back and forth between the drinking Yupa and the trough, to fill and refill, fetch and deliver one calabash of *chicha* after another. Even this service, as I have seen it performed, is carried out by the pygmoids with serenity, and it probably has some ceremonial significance. Never, however, have I seen them participate as equals in the drinking spree, with its dancing, singing, fighting, and yelling. They just stand quietly around the beer trough and drink. No one has ever reported hearing them sing. "Los pigmoides nunca cantaban," writes Laffer (1959:8), "aunque les pidiesen hacerlo. En todo lo demás eran prontos para complacerlo."

With an average body weight of a little over one hundred pounds, the pygmoids bound through the difficult terrain of their environment like so many mountain goats. Their agility makes them welcome allies or formidable foes in time of war. As the Yupa put it: the white man is easy to kill because he can't see

Figure 1: Calabashes used as drinking cups.

us with his blue eyes, but the Pïpïntu move quickly and sometimes we can't see them. "Wir sahen sie nicht kommen, wir sehen keine Bewegung an Ihnen. Sie stehen einfach da vor der grünen Wand," writes a surprised Vareschi (1959:87).

Characteristically, the pygmoids are retiring and communicate in brief signals and subdued voices. They seem to despise and ridicule the verbosity of their masters. Usually they sit by as keen but silent observers. "The Yupa," says Laffer (1959:7), "are chatterboxes, and usually by nightfall they converse a lot with high-pitched voices and frequent laughter. The pygmoids participate in the gatherings and pay great attention to what is said, but they never conducted discussions on their own."

I have sat with pygmoids and Yupa together in the same camp, but never have I heard the pygmoids speak to one another. The Yupa assured me that the pygmoids speak Yupan, which is no doubt the case. We do not know for certain, however, whether they also use Yupan among themselves. Vareschi (1959:88) observed that, "keiner unserer Begleiter vemag die Sprache der kleinen Kerle richtig zu verstehen." It may be, however, that the Yupan of his guides and the Yupan of the pygmoids were mutually unintelligible. An Irapa, for example, cannot understand a Japreria. Thus we do not know whether the pygmoids are bilingual, but it would not be surprising to find that an aboriginal language had been completely replaced by Yupan. Not only would this be in good "pygmy" tradition, it would also resemble the case of the Yupan-speaking Irapa who, according to Villamañan (1959:233), are "una tribu marginal asimilada por los caribes . . . Emplean aún muchas palabras diversas como sinónimos." Here again, we do not know about the possible existence of such "synonyms" in the language of the pygmoid Yupa. For the time being, we can only accept Pineda's (1945:350) statement that "el idioma de estos indígenas de baja estatura es asimismo un dialecto karib, fuertemente emparentado con los Opón-Carare, karib de gran estatura."

Notwithstanding their condition of semiservitude to the taller Yupa, the pygmoids continue to live in their own family units wherever possible. While it is true that the women often serve the Yupa men as concubines, they nevertheless rejoin the pygmoid men in the evening and stay with them until daybreak and for as long during the day as circumstance will permit. The women weave in front of their huge vertical looms, the men may work on a new pot or pipe, or the couple may leave the settlement to tend to their fields, which invariably are better kept than those of the taller Yupa.

Before leaving the settlement the pygmoid man will check and retouch his facial paint. Painting the face is of significance among the Yupa, but the colors and designs used by the pygmoids appear to differ from those of the Yupa. One of the earlier reliable sources reports, "black, brown, and scarlet pigments" (de Booy 1918b:198) in use by precontact and premission Yupa. The pygmoids prefer black, and they blacken large parts of their faces without showing much interest in the symbolic geometrical designs used by the other Yupa.

The Yupa themselves are outspoken about the physical and cultural differences that exist between them and the small people they call Pïpïntu. Their tale *In the Land of the Dwarfs* (8) is explicit on the differences in origin, physiognomy, and behavior of the Pïpïntu. The pygmoids come from a subterranean world where the excrement of the terrestrial Yupa falls on their heads and causes the baldness of the bearded dwarfs. They nourish themselves by inhaling clouds of smoke from their fires, and enjoy solid food by letting it slide down their spines. They cannot ingest the food because they lack digestive tracts, and consequently have no anuses. They are friendly, honest, peace-loving people, who enjoy dancing around their fires. They were discovered by a Yupa whom they begged to operate on them, so as to give them an anus. Although these attempts failed, the small people let the Yupa return to earth and gave him a woman as his companion. The terrestrial pygmoids are the hybrid descendants of this mixed marriage.

This peculiar tale of the origin of the Yupa Pïpïntu seems to belong to a rare type reported from only a few places in the world (Thompson 1932–1936:137), in widely separated areas, most of which are known to be the habitat of contemporary pygmoid peoples. The tale and its component motifs remain surprisingly uniform. Norbeck (1955:62–69) reported on its occurrence in the Pacific and in the New World.

These trans-Pacific folkloristic similarities are of considerable culture-historical interest in relation to the Yupa pygmoids. In the Americas the story of subterranean people with the aforementioned characteristics was recorded from Panajachel, Guatemala,[1] from the Chamí of the Chocó, Colombia,[2] from the Catío immediately to the east of the Chocó,[3] from the Yupa of Colombia and Venezuela,[4] and from the Yanoama (Sanemá) of Venezuela.[5] A closely related story has also been recorded among the Warao of Venezuela,[6] and the Shipaya of the Xingú.[7] The Yupa version herein (8) represents probably the most complete and detailed example of this type of tale in the New World.

As to its occurrence in the Pacific, the tale has become known from Luzon and interior Formosa, more specifically from the Apayao* and the Atayal.**

As Norbeck (1955:62) notes, both Nordenskiöld and Wassén have done considerable work on the similarities that apparently exist in the folklore of the Americas and of various areas of the Pacific. In most instances one cannot rule out independent origins, but in the case of the tradition of the underworld people, and several of its component motifs, Norbeck, who found the same tale in mountain Luzon and interior Formosa, thought it suggested "an interpretation other than independent development" (ibid). According to him "it seems improbable that the coincidences in motifs are simply fortuitous" (ibid).

It is interesting, as pointed out, that most of the areas from which the stories have been reported are inhabited by pygmoid peoples. The Sierra de Perijá, in particular, and northwestern South America in general, are known as distribution areas of pygmoid Indians. The Yanoama (Sanemá) have a minority pygmoid component with a general stature of less than 130 cm (Zerries 1959) living among them. The hinterland of Luzon is the home of the Pinatubo Negritos, and the land of the Apayaos, from which the tale has been specifically reported, is inhabited by people among whom "physically, the Indonesian strains dominate; but

---

[1] Tax 1951:2657
[2] Chaves 1945:145–146; Reichel-Dolmatoff 1953:165; Norbeck 1955:64
[3] Rochereau 1929:100–101
[4] Wilbert 1962b:864–866
[5] Wilbert 1963:234
[6] Roth 1915:126 ff.
[7] Nimuendajú 1919–1920:1022

*Wilson 1947:88
**Norbeck 1950:14–15

mongoloid features of all the three short types are present, especially the short Mongols" (Wilson 1947:1).

Further, it is noteworthy that the narrators of the Philippine story who were short themselves make no particular mention of the fact that the subterranean people were dwarfs, unless the reference to their "very light bodies" in the Atayal story is intended to convey this meaning. It is in the New World that the underworld people become dwarfs, and the story with its "extraordinary" people is employed to rationalize a strange phenomenon of their tribal life: the existence of "midgets" among them. The Yupa and Chami, who have had to wrestle intellectually with this fact of life, are the only American peoples to adopt the Apayao motif of the successful operation, together with the rationalization that "normal" offspring may result from the union of a pygmoid person and his/her "normal" mate. This particular story may have been adopted in all its detail by either the Philippine natives or by the New World Indians because it satisfied the intellectual need to cope with the specific human phenomenon of exceptional smallness. In the Philippine tale the solution of the problem hinges on a clinical intervention, while the Yupa and Chami versions introduce the almost too rational notion of hybridization in order to account for the presence of pygmoids in their world.

Supposing that for the sake of argument, we are faced in this instance of tale-motif distribution with trait diffusion rather than independent invention, one might turn, especially in view of the geographical distribution, to the available sources on the trans-Pacific Manila Galleon trade route, which for two and a half centuries, between 1565 and 1815, connected Mexico and the Philippines with a thin but enduring chain of exchanges. To be sure, the annual average of one to three vessels did not make for large-scale traffic, but it was traffic in the right direction, and the diffusion of a tale type does not require a large number of people.

Hinterland Filipinos and Indians in Mexico, Guatemala, Colombia, Peru, and Venezuela, all lived within the direct or indirect sphere of influence of the Manila Galleon trade, and there is evidence that both Filipinos and Indians were directly involved in it. According to Norbeck (1955:66), Friede and Reichel-Dolmatoff have discovered "Spanish documents dealing with the transporting of Colombian Indians to the Philippines during the eighteenth century." To my knowledge, these documents have not yet been published, but it is likely that such movement took place in connection with the Manila Galleon trade. The transport of groups of Indians under Spanish domain occurred frequently and on an almost worldwide basis. "When the first galleon trade was inaugurated between Manila and Acapulco, the Spaniards employed Filipino crews to man the ships that made the yearly profitable arrivals and departures of Manila-Mexico vessels of fortune. The Filipinos who were aboard these sailing vessels all spoke Tagalog" (Verzosa 1940:37–38). A number of them remained in the New World and spread from Mexico to South America, from Colombia to Venezuela, and even to Cuba. The establishment of the coconut wine industry through the agency of Filipino Indians, as the aboriginal crew members of the galleons were called, is a good example of the impact of cultural diffusion on New World Indian societies, as well as on non-Indian inhabitants. Bruman (1945:216) quotes the following pertinent passage from Blair and Robertson (1903–1909, 18:184–185):

. . . there are in Nueva España so many of those Indians who came from the Filipinas Islands who have engaged in making palm wine along the other seacoast, that of the South Sea, and which they make with stills, as in Filipinas, that it will in time become a part reason for the natives of Nueva España who now use the wine that comes from Castilla, to drink none except what the Filipinos make. For since the natives of Nueva España are a race inclined to drink and intoxication, and the wine made by the Filipinos is distilled and as strong as brandy, they crave it rather than the wine from España. . . . So great is the traffic in this [palm wine] at present on the coast at Navidad, among the Apusabalcos, and throughout Colima, that they load beasts of burden with this wine in the same way as in España. By postponing the speedy remedy that this demands, the same thing might also happen to the vineyards of Piru. It can be averted, provided all the Indian natives of the said Filipinas Islands are shipped and returned to them, that the palm groves and vessels with which the wine is made be burnt, the palm-trees felled, and severe penalties imposed on whomever remains or returns to make that wine.

Incited by their greed in that traffic, all the Indians who have charge of making that wine go to the port of Acapulco when the ships reach there from Manila, and lead away with them all the Indians who come as common seamen. For that reason, and the others above mentioned, scarcely any of them return to the said Filipinas Islands. . . . In the galleon "Espiritu Santo" which came last year, six hundred and eighteen, were seventy-five native Indians as common seamen, but not more than five of the entire number returned in the said galley.

Bruman (1945:217) found the name for coconut wine in western Mexico to be *tuba* which is Filipino (Tagalog), rather than Indian or Spanish, and he refers to a previous publication (1944:418–427) in which he cited evidence that in addition to coconut wine "the Filipinos introduced a number of traits into Western Mexico that became thoroughly integrated into mestizo and even tribal culture." Among the more noteworthy of these were several types of Asiatic stills for the making of strong alcoholic beverages (Bruman (1945:215).

For further evidence of the impact of American Indian cultures on the Filipinos, one need only think of the phenomenal diffusion of useful New World plants. "In 1912, Merill noted that at least 178 species of plants had been introduced either purposely or accidentally from the New World. Over 100 of these were apparently brought between the years 1512 and 1815 from Mexico by the Spaniards on the annual galleons" (Fox 1952:193). Some fifty New World plants are found within the Pinatubo Negrito territory, and all but four are used in some manner by the pygmies. Among these cultigens are potatoes, maize, bitter manioc, and tobacco. Fox (1952:246) estimates that approximately 70 percent of the Pinatubo pygmies' present food is derived from plants introduced into Luzon from the New World since the Spanish Conquest.

Plants that are not used for food are also utilized in the Philippines exactly as they are in the New World. It appears, for example, that the Pinatubo pygmies of Luzon became especially fond of tobacco, once the plant had been introduced from America. "All pygmies are heavy smokers. It is commonplace to see even six-year-old boys and girls smoking large, green-leafed cigars" (Fox 1952:196). Not only does nonritual, excessive smoking of tobacco by young and old alike exhibit an interesting parallel between the Yupa and Negritos, but both peoples rely equally heavily on extensive pharmaceutical knowledge in curing illnesses. In contrast, curing practices in South America are based largely on shamanism—that is, treatment is primarily by supernatural means. Only in the Andean highlands are medicinal plants more extensively employed.

The Yupa can name and describe hundreds of plants and explain their utility to man. Such knowledge is general in the tribe, but men and women who are exceptional in this respect are called *tuano**. Both the office and the term are non-Carib and atypical for Neo-Indian societies of lowland South America. The pygmies of Luzon are also famous for their botanical and pharmaceutical abilities. They know "specific or descriptive names of at least 450 plants. . . ." (Fox 1952:188). Their medicine man (or woman), known as *mananámbal,* uses plants constantly in curing séances. These sessions are called *ani-tuwán,* a word that appears to be in part cognate with the Yupa *tuano.* Similar forms, with the meaning "master" or, in a more general sense, "a person of distinction," occur as *tuan* (Sea Dayak), *tuwan* (Java), *tuwani* (Galela, Halmahera), *tuan* (Standard Malay) of wider Indonesian-Malayan distribution. It thus seems possible that the Yupan *tuano* is a foreign name for an unusual occupation, just as forms of Mexican-Indian terms are used for various plants and cultural goods in the Philippines (Zingg 1934:251).

Here is not the place to examine in detail the folklore of the two regions, Pacific and Latin American, nor is there space to consider in depth the problem of movement of aboriginal groups between Luzon and Formosa in the Pacific and Colombia and Guatemala in the New World during the Colonial period. The limited data cited thus far, however, should be of interest to ethnologists working in both areas in that it contains clues to a number of problems related to culture-trait diffusion between the populations of the Pacific and the Indians of Latin America.

It is difficult to determine the direction in which our particular tale type might have diffused. Norbeck (1955:67) considers it unlikely "that the motif in question reached the mountain peoples of Luzon through the agency of Colombian Indians. Such an hypothesis would shed no light on Formosan folklore, and the similarity in mythology between Formosa and mountain Luzon appears very much closer than between either of these areas and Colombia." In light of available data the same cannot be maintained for the American side. There were contacts between Gua-

---

*Hildebrandt (1958:70) explains the entry *tuánu* or *tuwáno* as *"mago, hechicero, brujo";* and in its extended meaning as *"diestro o docto en algo."*

temala and Colombia in pre-Hispanic and post-Conquest times; accordingly cultural traits diffused from Mexico down the Pacific coast of Central America and South America. The greatest similarity exists among Yupa, Chocó, Panajachel, and Pacific tales. (It does not shed much light on Sanemá and Warao mythology, nor, for that matter on the Adji of the Shipaya, but western South American traits are not unusual among Venezuelan tribes.) At present, therefore, "it seems more reasonable to conjecture that at least some of the American Indians transported to the Philippines were later returned to South America and resumed life with their own or other American tribal groups." There is also the possibility that the tale was diffused to the New World by Filipinos from the region of the Apayaos, where, as we saw, it has been recorded.

THE EUROPEANS FROM ACROSS THE SEA

Situated in the northwestern corner of South America, the Sierra de Perijá belongs to the regions of the New World that were explored almost immediately after Discovery. Columbus had hardly reached the New World in 1498 when Amérigo Vespucci and Alonso de Ojeda sailed along the North Coast (1499–1550), reaching the western shore of the Guajira Peninsula, adjacent to Yupa territory. They were followed by Juan Ampies (1527), who founded the town of Santa Ana de Coro. The Welsers of Augsburg obtained the territory of Venezuela from Charles V in 1529, and the exploratory expeditions of their various commanders such as Alfinger and Federmann began as early as 1530.

In 1550 Alonso Pérez de Tolosa made contact with the Indians of the Sierra. But only between 1779 and 1792 did the Capuchin missionaries of Navarra and Cantabria succeed in collecting several Yupa groups known as Chaque and Motilones into small settlements within the northern and southern sections of the mountain range. According to an 1810 census, there were ten missions with a total of 1,190 Indians. Relations between the Indians and the whites were cool and hostile almost from the beginning; they deteriorated completely after 1836 when the Indians were severely provoked through hostile acts by the whites. They withdrew into the mountains, declaring war to the death on all "Pañur," that is Spaniards or whites (Jahn 1927; Métraux and Kirchhoff 1948).

The advent of the white man must have seemed like a nightmare to the Indians, who lacked tactics and means to cope with these creatures from across the sea. The so-called "undeclared war" against the Indians of Venezuela began precisely in the Maracaibo area with the first *entradas* out of Santa Ana de Coro. Chief objective was the discovery of a fabled Eldorado somewhere in the mountainous hinterlands of Coro, in the Cordilleras east and west of Lake Maracaibo, or in the Meta region. These forays resulted in the devastation of extensive, densely populated areas of northern Venezuela and of adjacent Colombia. For instance, on his *entrada* to Valledupar, the German Alfinger razed the settlements that lay along his bloody trail so completely that his compatriot, Nicolaus Federmann, who later covered the same route, found the entire region devoid of Indian life. In his greed for gold Alfinger imprisoned hundreds upon hundreds of Indians in stockades, where they were left to starve to death unless ransomed by their relatives. The Zapara, who lived on the eastern shore of Lake Maracaibo opposite the location of the modern city of Maracaibo, were wholly annihilated. Georg Hohermuth had the dubious distinction of depopulating the entire Valle de las Damas by systematically massacring the tribes of Barquisimeto and Acarigua. Federmann, following the custom of the day, punished all who refused to supply his army, present him with gifts, or serve either as burden bearers or cannon fodder on his expedition to Acarigua and beyond. Whole villages were systematically put to the torch, for instance those of the Cuyones on the headwaters of the Portuguesa, in Jirajara country. On one occasion, under pretext of negotiating for peace, Federmann (1965:77) ordered an attack on the Guaycaries; his soldiers stabbed them "like pigs" and five hundred perished in the massacre.

These are but a few statistics of the "undeclared war" against the Indians in Venezuela, news of which might have reached the Yupa as it did the other Indians in the general region. And like the Indians of the Andes east of Lake Maracaibo, the Yupa managed to flee into the most inaccessible mountain reaches where, as Federmann (1965:80) himself was forced to admit, "one could not follow them on cats, let alone on horses." No wonder, then, that Yupa folk literature describes the origin and history of the white man as another critical period in tribal history which provoked the creator to intervene in man's affairs.

The mother of the white man was conceived in an abnormal fashion—by a Yupa woman masturbating with an artificial phallus. Discovering the secret, members of the tribe shattered the stone to pieces and the deprived woman died of grief over her dead "husband" (10).

The girl that resulted from this union became so embittered at her fellowmen that she set out to destroy them all. At the age of three she invented machines, iron tools, and guns and she would have carried on with her plan had the creator not found it necessary to intervene.

In the story of his intervention "god" is depicted as a careful judge and a fair being who looked with anxious eyes on the doings of the girl. On the one hand he did not want her to carry out her plan to annihilate the tribe, on the other hand he was far from pleased with what he knew to be the intentions of the Yupa, who, fearing the girl because of her magical arts, had decided to kill her. As in the creation story (1), "god" again employs the services of a bird, this time King Vulture, to facilitate his plan of separating the hostile parties.

The girl journeyed across the ocean and, while she was walking over the waters, the sea made her pregnant. She reached the European continent where she gave birth to a son, the first white man, whose ancestors include his grandmother, a Yupa; his grandfather, a stone; his mother illegitimate, and his father, the sea. The boy grew up and fathered many children through intercourse with his own mother, his sisters, and his daughters. And that is how the white race came into existence. The Europeans continued to manufacture the same iron weapons as their ancestor, and all their inventions and tools are created for one purpose only: eventually to destroy the Indians. In 1492 they had finally come to Yupa country to carry out their plans.

Around 1915 relations between Indians and whites began to improve somewhat. The Capuchins started their second mission campaign at La Granja, on the Colombian side of the Sierras, and more recently, in 1945, at Los Angeles del Tucucu, on the Venezuelan side. But even today, many Yupa remain skeptical and shun any rapprochement. They know their myth of the origin of the whites and their technology all too well. All too distinctly do they recall their traditional history lessons that describe the trials of their ancestors, whom the Europeans drove up into the mist-shrouded mountains, when there remained no place for them but the clouds. What can persuade them to believe that the whites have finally abandoned their sinister plans of genocide and ethnocide? Who guarantees them a life in peace in accordance with the ancestral design?

THE PROMISED LAND

It seems that at least for now the Yupa prefer to place more trust in the promised land that awaits all Yupa after death than in the white man. Narrative 6 gives us a fairly detailed description of its geography.

The Land of the Dead is located on the same plane as the Land of the Living. The two are separated by a zone of transition, an area from which the souls of recently deceased people may once more return to the Land of the Living to see to one thing or another before departing forever from this world. The path to the Land of the Dead leads through a perilous forest, a fortified wall and, finally, across a wide river.

In the forest the wandering soul eventually reaches the house of Kopecho. We met this mythical woman on a previous occasion (2), before her transformation into a frog or toad. It was she who, through her sensuous dancing, lured one of the two suns then existing into a fire pit, thereby not only transforming it into the moon but also initiating the cycle of day and night—that is, time. In Yupa lore the frog woman is thus intimately related to the night, the moon, and the water. Her house in the zone of testing and transition between the land of the living and that of the dead is situated at the junction of two roads, that of the good souls and that of the bad. It may also be the intersection where Indian lore meets the Christian tradition of purgatory.

Indigenous, I would suggest, is the test of the soul's proficiency in basketmaking. It is a well-known fact that the Carib, much like other Indians of the tropical forest, are expert basket weavers, among whom basketry products are in constant demand. An accomplished basket weaver enjoys considerable prestige as an artisan and as a good provider for his family. For centuries baskets have represented a desirable stock-in-trade for intertribal commerce. Less well known than these technical and socioeconomic aspects of indigenous basket weaving are those that transcend earthly considerations and relate the artisan to the metaphysical and to his life after death.

Among the Yecuana, for instance, it goes without saying that an old basket weaver knows how to edge the various types of baskets properly and has mastered the proportions for different diameters. What is much more important is that he can freely apply his technical skills to create significant representations of the real Yecuana in two-dimensional form. This is particularly important for the weaving of zoomorphic designs onto the surface of rectangular storage baskets and round trays. These designs, passed on from one generation to the next, symbolize metaphysical content and are derived from Yecuana mythology. The thematic content and execution are discussed with concentration among the artisans, who depict a large part of their ideology in more than thirty major classes of such metaphysical motifs, including representations of the constellations, the water snake, the mythical Sacred Monkey who brought yuca into the world, and the frog. From this it is not difficult to derive a strong motivation for a native to master the art of basketry to perfection, to provide for his status in this life and his role in the transmission of tribal ideology in the service of the supernatural powers (Wilbert 1972a:125).

An even stronger case for the physical and metaphysical importance of basketry in indigenous lore is provided by the Warao Indians. At the risk of going too far afield I would, nevertheless, point out that baskets play a very important role in Warao culture, from a technical as well as socioeconomic point of view. Again, however, of equal importance are the metaphysical beliefs intimately associated with the art of basket weaving. Through the continuous handling of the *sehoro* reed, the spirit of *sehoro* converts the expert into a *sehoro* (light)-shaman. The spirit appears in the artisan's dream and hands him a cigar and a set of tutelary spirits (Wilbert 1972b:65–72). This gift, which makes the basketry-shaman equal to the light shaman of the Warao, is the distinction that also marks the *uasi,* the expert weaver. He is transformed into a religious practitioner by virtue of practicing his art. Throughout his life he provides his people with all the baskets they need and, in return, is rewarded with the gift of shamanic powers. Even beyond the grave he will remain a chosen one, for his soul will dwell with the divine Bird of the Dawn in the company of the many *uasi* basketry experts who went before him.

Whether a soul will reach this happy destination or be made to suffer torments is determined by Kopecho, the Yupa Mistress of Frogs, on the basis of the quality of basketry the souls weave as they make their way along the path to the Otherworld. What I intended by way of the Yecuana and Warao examples is to show that basketry may be so highly valued in native lore that at least in some societies it is actually the degree of skill and artistry applied to this craft that determines man's final destiny after death. It is therefore entirely possible that, notwithstanding superficial resemblances to Christian concepts of divine judgment, Kopecho, in her role as arbiter of the soul's fate, may have been placed on the path to the Otherworld by the Indians themselves, rather than through the influence of Christian missionaries of the eighteenth century.*

Character and function of the next station on the way to the world of the dead may strike the reader as less than autochthonous, because it seems to adapt to the indigenous experience the sort of torment ascribed to sinners in the Christian hell. A soul that produces satisfactory basketry is sent by Kopecho along the path to the Land of the Dead. In contrast, the soul of the inept basket weaver is sent to a river on which there rolls a huge, hollow tree that reaches from shore to shore. The path leads directly into this log and, within it, the souls of the "bad" Yupa are tumbled about, to be clawed and devoured by wild beasts. While this certainly sounds like a version of hell or purgatory, it may also have its origin in the familiar clashing rocks, snapping jaws, and other perilous passages in funerary and shamanist mythologies.**

Next the path through the perilous forest leads the soul to a wall that bounds the Land of the Dead. Any soul that passed Kopecho's basketry test may take up the big cudgel he finds

*Kopecho is the Yupa version of Toad Grandmother as Mistress of the Earth and the Underworld. Among the Tacana of Bolivia she herself devours the dead, just as does Tlaltecuhtli, the personification of the earth as a monstrous toad in Aztec Mexico.

**The Yupa tradition of the spinning hollow log is reminiscent of a perilous passage that, according to the Guarayú, the soul has to clear on its journey to the land of the Great Ancestors. It has to jump and balance on a tree trunk which floats at great speed back and forth between the shores of the river of the Otherworld (Métraux 1948:437). One is also reminded of the "snake log" of the Chippewa Indians of North America (Barnouw 1973:296, 388).

leaning against the wall and with it force a passage through this formidable barrier to the other side.

After passing through the wall the soul comes to the bank of a wide river. He is carried across the water by holding on to a huge dog. This water constitutes the dividing line between the Land of the Living and an intermediate zone from the Land of the Dead. Here the soul of the Yupa live in harmony and happiness, conducting "themselves exactly as do the living" (6).

Manufacturing and Building

PROCESSING THE BASIC MATERIALS

The Yupa work neither stone nor leather. They fashion arrowheads out of bone or scrap iron. Men are good basket weavers and fashion satchels, telescoping boxes, quivers, and fire fans in twilled and hexagonal weaves. Men also employ the coiling technique to make crude cooking pots with pointed bottoms and two or four ears. The ware is decorated with finger impressions rather than paint.

Noteworthy in Yupa material culture are pipes composed of a clay bowl and a wooden stem. They are made by the men but used by both men and women, even children (see fig. 7). In the folk literature potter's clay is personfied as a companion of Tapir (40). They became separated and while the Tapir now travels with the *coruba* and the royal palms in the lowlands, Clay stayed with the Yupa up in the mountains, where he produced "a number of black and white clay pipes as well as containers of the most varied sort." Ethnographically it is likely that the Yupa began making clay pipes after they had moved into the Sierra.

Yupa women spin cotton and weave tunic-like garments for their menfolk as well as skirts for themselves. Vertical looms were operated by Yupa women when they were first contacted by twentieth-century field workers. It is possible that the large vertical loom was of limited distribution among the Yupa subtribes,

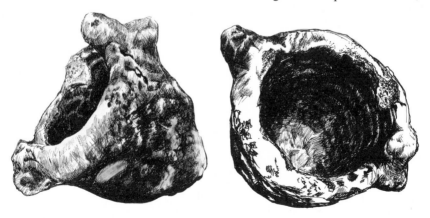

Figure 2: Crude cooking pot made in the coiling technique.

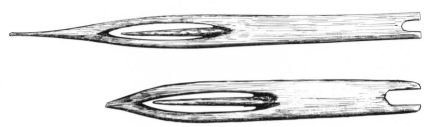

Figure 3: Wooden "sword" used by the women to drive down the weft on their vertical looms.

whereas the narrow frame loom found among the Barí to the south came to be more generally accepted (Bolinder 1925:234, fig. 76). The large loom is atypical of Carib culture, and the Yupa probably adopted it from their western Andean neighbors subsequent to their migration into the Sierra de Perijá. Since the missions have introduced clothing there is no longer a need for weaving, and the fabric that is occasionally still manufactured

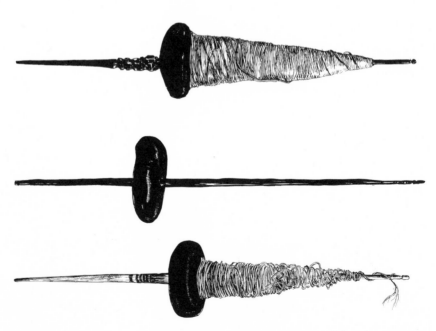

Figure 4: Spindles with plain and decorated shafts used by the women to spin cotton in the so-called Bacairi technique. The shafts are ca. 30 cm long and the whorls are discs made of stone.

by Yupa women is of inferior quality. At present it is mainly the pygmoid women who make good cloth, a fact that confirms the general impression that it is the small-statured Yupa who are the expert craftsmen among these Indians.

HOUSES AND SETTLEMENTS

The members of a particular Yupa subtribe may reside together in single homesteads, in hamlets of two or three houses, or in larger settlements of more than ten houses. Yupa shelters are not too well adapted to the weather conditions of their present mountain habitat. The often wall-less houses are rectangular in shape and are covered with palm-frond roofs. But frequently a Yupa shelter is no more than a simple lean-to, or two lean-tos with enclosed ends and a small porch along the front. The Indians sleep on a pad of ferns and mats; hammocks are absent. Each hut normally shelters a nuclear family.

In the folk literature the reader is twice introduced to houses of a different kind. The souls in the *Land of the Dead* (6) are said to live in villages of round huts, reminiscent of Kogi or Ica settlements or, indeed, of the round communal dwellings of Cariban and other Neo-Indians of the Tropical Forest. Such a dwelling of the *churuata* or *maloka* type might also have served as prototype for the huge house with thick walls of leaves which the shaman of another story (9) built for his entire group.

Making a Living

GROWING FOOD

In the past, field workers have expressed contradictory opinions regarding the relative importance of cultivated plants among the Yupa. Bolinder (1917:30) speaks of very large fields and even *gewaltige Urbarmachungen,* whereas Reichel-Dolmatoff (1945:29) has been little impressed by the "rudimentary and deficient agriculture" of the Yuco in Colombia. Similarly, the La Salle expedition (Sociedad de Ciencias Naturales La Salle 1953:62) refers to only incipient horticulture among the Venezuelan Yupa. Notwithstanding these impressionistic judgments and despite the fact that, as Gusinde (1965a:202) pointed out, the Yupa can expect to reap only a "nominal harvest," there can be no doubt that compared with other food sources slash-and-burn agriculture represents the most important single factor in the food economy of these Indians (Ruddle, 1970a:54).

According to Santelos (1959–1960:243) every Yupa would mention sweet manioc, plantain, maize, yam, and pigeon pea as the five crops recognized as "basic" by the Yupa. Recent studies (Ruddle 1970a) have shown a more comprehensive inventory of fifty-two crops including sweet yuca, *ocumo,* canna, yam, squash, sweet potato, chili pepper, maize, bean, pigeon pea, plantain, banana, sugarcane, and papaya. This is an impressive variety and Reichel-Dolmatoff is correct in his judgment that the Yupa food supply is basically vegetable (Fernández Yepez 1945:67; Gusinde 1956a:202). Yet, variety does not necessarily mean abundance, so that "the problem of food [remains] a matter of constant concern ..." (Holder 1947:423), and the possibility of a famine, as punishment for disregarding the incest taboo, for instance, an ever present anxiety (15).

Each nuclear family owns at least one or two small fields, which are cleared by the men and planted by both sexes. Harvesting is largely done by the women.

The wide variety of cultivated crops notwithstanding, the real staples of Yupa horticulture are sweet yuca and maize. In sharp contrast with the eastern Cariban tribes of Venezuela, the Yupa do not plant the bitter variety of manioc.

30

The Yupa ascribe the original ownership of yuca, batata, yams, and bananas to the Moon. From him a hunter received the plants as "a gift to the human beings on earth" (7, 42). Upon his return to earth, goes the story, the man introduced the crops to the people according to the instructions Moon had given him. Before this, the Yupa lived mainly off the animals in the forest and, according to the origin story of maize (41), they also collected a wild-growing tuber plant called *makahka*.

Among other innovations, the culture hero, Oséema, is credited with the introduction of maize and related practices. He arrived on earth as an adolescent boy for the express purpose of introducing mankind to the growing of maize. Oséema thoroughly disliked the wild-growing *makahka*. Before he finally found a group of humans to whom to give the maize, he secretly prepared a daily ration of *tuka*, a maize drink for himself, simply because he could not stand the taste of *makahka*. Nor did he eat of the batata, yams, or bananas that sprang up wherever he urinated.

Oséema carried the maize kernels in his head.* The first humans who, according to the story (41), ever saw the maize were a group of hospitable women. Thrilled with the music, heretofore never heard, which the hero and his companions evoked from a pair of special clarinets (fig. 10), the women had succeeded in persuading the wandering musicians to linger. It was they who, in the course of the following night, were chosen by Oséema to become the first recipients of maize. He taught them how to plant, harvest, and process the cereal. When their menfolk returned they too agreed to adopt the new food in favor of the wild *makahka,* and even today, long after the departure of the culture hero, the Yupa, before they cut a new crop of maize, blow "upon the instruments of Oséema, that he may always grant them an abundant harvest."**

In the oral literature, then, we encounter a contradictory origin for batata, yam, and banana, which are ascribed at the same time

*This peculiarity, together with the fact that Oséema is described as an attractive young person, makes the Yupa culture hero resemble the maize god of the Maya. "He was probably not only the god of maize, but a general agricultural deity. He is always pictured as youthful and handsome, and usually has a maize plant sprouting from his head or headdress" (Benson 1967:115).

**Oséema was forced to leave the Yupa because his companion accidentally spilled maize on the ground. This is considered a serious matter and as such is reminiscent of the behavior of the Maya of Zinacantan who will lap up spilled *atole* and collect even one fallen kernel of maize, which is considered to have a soul, rather than allow it to rot on the ground (Vogt 1969:35).

to Moon and to Oséema. While such mythic discrepancies may not always require an explanation, in this case one may be possible. Oséema and associated beliefs about maize are strongly related to the Irapa subtribe of the Yupa. Considering the cultural differences between the Irapa and the rest of the Yupa population, it is possible that in this instance we are dealing with the effects of two different traditions that came to overlap, and that eventually yuca belongs to Moon and maize to Oséema (Wilbert 1959:138).

Besides yuca, batata, and bananas Moon is also supposed to have given man the first cottonseeds (7). Ethnographers have reported wild cotton growing in the cloud forests of Perijá, but it is more likely to be an escape plant that requires no special care once it has grown to sufficient size.

USEFUL PLANTS AND FOOD COLLECTING

Cotton is not the only plant kept by the Yupa as a source of either raw material or supplementary food. Other such important plants are indigo, maguey, *onoto,* castor bean, coca, and gourd. The trees include calabash, cacao, *caimito,* guama, jobo, lime, *mamón,* algarroba, and tamarind. Tobacco is also grown by the Yupa, among whom, as noted, both sexes, and even children, are avid pipe smokers.

Generally speaking, the collecting of edible materials is of major economic importance for the Yupa. In addition to fruits, seeds, and vegetables, they also gather insects, larvae, crabs, snails, the eggs of birds and reptiles, and honey. Snails are considered a choice food (19).

HUNTING

The Yupa are excellent hunters and many kinds of birds and mammals contribute substantially to their diet.

With the exception of birds of prey, the Yupa hunt whatever fowl frequents the Sierra de Perijá, from the tiny hummingbird to the large *pava.* Hummingbirds are shot with very fine arrows, and the hunter sets out to shoot from fifteen to twenty of them at a time. Even in such quantities, hummingbirds remain a special tidbit. They are roasted on small sticks and eaten with plantains (Santelos 1959–1960:6). The very light *omaye* arrow is used mainly to hunt birds of larger size. Preferred are turkeys, macaws, parrots, toucans, pigeons of the forest and of the mountains, tinamous, and others. As mentioned, the eggs of all these birds are collected and eaten boiled.

To get as close as possible to the birds, the Yupa build blinds high in the tops of trees known to be special feeding places for certain birds. They may also set up a tepee-like pole construction close to a fruit-bearing tree and build the blind on this (Hitchcock 1954:15, fig. 17). Accompanied by his wife, the hunter leaves his house as early as three in the morning in order to be in his blind by four, shortly before the birds arrive to feed on the tree. He has his bamboo quiver full of *omaye* arrows handy and shoots birds one by one as they arrive. His wife collects them at intervals at the foot of the tree (Bolinder 1925:225; Fernández Yepez 1945:68; Sociedad de Ciencias Naturales La Salle 1953:60).

Similar blinds are also set up on the ground. To attract the birds, the hunter baits the area near his hideout with maize kernels, bananas, and honeycombs with larvae in them. He also attracts the birds very effectively by imitating their calls. In the dry season the hunter takes up his position close to a water hole. It is surprising that the Yupa, who must rely heavily on fowling, do not seem to have developed any special bird-catching techniques, such as the use of nets, snares, or birdlime, or at least none have so far come to my attention. Instead, they have specialized in bow-and-arrow hunting techniques and have developed special arrows and accessories related to them—for example, the multipronged *omaye* arrow, blinds, baiting techniques, and birdcalls.

Small rodents like rats and squirrels are hunted with skill and persistence. All mice and rats are eaten, but the Yupa take special delight in hunting the field mice that frequent their maize plots and grain storage huts. To catch them, the hunter places bait close to a pile of resinous seeds called *kate,* which he lights in the evening and which will cast a pale light on the nearby bait. He takes his position a short distance away, waiting for the mice with a small *mápiche* arrow on his bowstring. It is reported that for better results, the hunter will sometimes keep the waxed arrow-tip hot (Santelos 1959–1960:325). *Picure* and *paca* are hunted in similar fashion, with a bait of maize or plantain. The hunter allows the rodents to eat their fill and shoots them when they start retreating. For these larger species, the small *mápiche* arrow, used on mice and smaller rodents, is replaced with a harpoon arrow, *tóyohka.* Should they escape wounded, the trailing string and arrow shaft will slow them down and betray their whereabouts. Another rodent, the squirrel, is frequently hunted with the *omaye* arrow. For this elusive animal the hunter will place a bait of maize kernels on a fallen tree trunk in the forest.

Different kinds of monkey occur in the Sierra de Perijá and all are hunted by the Yupa; they include *marimondo,* white-faced monkey, howler monkey, two unidentified species called *konuksha* (nocturnal monkey) and *koso;* and a nocturnal monkey called *pukshi.* The Yupa designate all these monkeys as *poroto,* the specific name for *marimondo,* probably because it is the latter species they like best. In describing the methods of hunting rodents, we have seen how the Yupa tries to slow the animal down by letting it eat its fill before he prepares to kill it. To hunt the agile monkey is certainly no less a task, and it is a rare hunter who all by himself succeeds in approaching his prey close enough to kill it. The *marimondos* travel in large groups, and as soon as their presence comes to the attention of the villagers several hunters team up for a drive. For this they select as the most adequate weapon the *míkivi* arrow, one of the largest in their arsenal (Santelos 1959–1960:327). The men surround the animals, which take refuge from the hunters high in the upper branches of the trees. If the men cannot shoot them from below, one of them will climb the tree to do so, while the others see to it that the monkeys do not escape the encirclement (Bañeres 1950:21–22). Like the monkey, the sloth is also killed with a large *míkivi.*

Although monkeys weighing three to nine kilograms can certainly be counted among the large-sized game hunted by the Yupa, there are even larger animals in the Sierra de Perijá, and a hunter never leaves the house without the hope that he may happen upon one of these. Among these are tapir, peccary, deer, and bear.

Usually the men prefer to hunt in twos and threes; friends may team up or a father may be accompanied by his sons (7). Since abduction of women has been practiced for centuries among the Yupa subtribes, however, the men are reluctant to leave their womenfolk unprotected. The culture hero Oséema, himself, chose to approach the Yupa village to carry out his plan at a time when the men had all gone on a hunt, leaving their women alone (41). That the women know how to take care of themselves is rather well described in the story of *An Attack of the Meteru* (14). The hunting down of a band of monkeys and drives of peccary often requires a collective effort of all able men (29). As the tale (42) explains, "hunting for wild boar [the men] surrounded a great number and drove them all together with loud shouts."

The main weapon of the Yupa hunter is the bow and arrow. A Pariri Indian once tried to describe to me a kind of trap that is employed (cf. Sociedad de Ciencias Naturales La Salle 1953:60), and a net trap, possibly connected with a deadfall, is also mentioned in the oral literature (42).

Most reptiles are caught and their eggs collected by the Yupa. Small children constantly chase iguanas, which the men shoot with small arrows (Bolinder 1917:31; 1925:226).

Except for the Irapa, several Yupa subtribes seem to observe a taboo against killing snakes. Gabaldon (1941:124) states that killing of reptiles was left to the children. Bolinder (1925:226) observed that southern Yupa rarely kill snakes preferring instead to sit down and let the reptiles pass. Should a Pariri hunter kill a snake accidentally or in self-defense, he will fast for several days and stay away from kitchen hearths and fireplaces. Under similar circumstances, Yupa of the Rio Negro subtribe must not light a fire or cook any food (Sociedad de Ciencias Naturals La Salle 1953:60).

Only the Irapa and the Maracá disregard all such proscriptions their fellow Yupa are concerned about. Santelos (1959–1960:6) writes that they capture snakes with a rope to the end of which is fastened a heavy pole approximately one meter long, which is lanced at the head of the serpent. Sometimes the Irapa lure the snake with a bird tied to the rope and kill the reptile when it is about to devour the bait. Often the snake gets entangled in the rope, enabling the hunter to shoot into its eyes arrows with hot resin tips. Only then do the hunters venture close enough to club the snake. They cut the reptile into pieces, roast the meat, and eat it with plantains or *ocumo*. Turtles and alligators are eaten by all Yupa. Toads and frogs, on the other hand, are associated with *Kopecho*, the mythical frog, and are not eaten (2, 6). Tabooed as a food source is also the opossum.

The Yupa are able imitators of animal calls. Although this is particularly true when it comes to bird calls, they are also adept at mimicking the calls of such animals as tapir and deer, and certain species of monkeys. By imitating the call of the jaguar

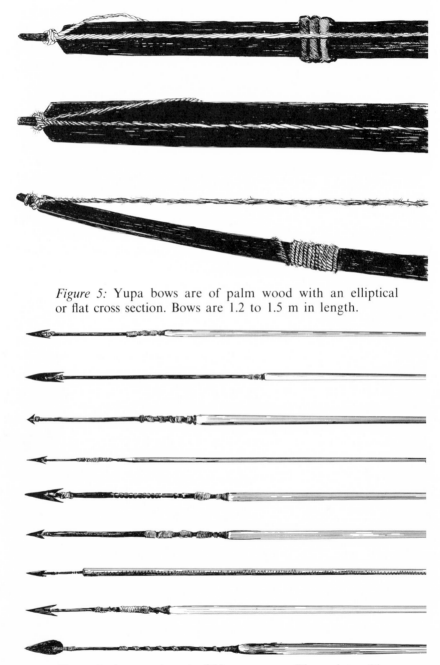

Figure 5: Yupa bows are of palm wood with an elliptical or flat cross section. Bows are 1.2 to 1.5 m in length.

Figure 6: An assortment of Yupa arrows. The points of iron or bone (far right) are perforated to facilitate a sturdy binding.

and puma they not only attract these animals but also lure others out of their hiding places. But the big cats themselves are not hunted by the Yupa and are killed only in self-defense. Usually the hunters use only their natural equipment to imitate animal calls, but for certain calls they may also employ leaves.*

Some beliefs and practices associated with hunting have been collected and observed among the Yupa over the years. By comparing these ethnographic data with the narrative material we may discover some of the underlying reasons for the various observances.

For example, snakes are generally avoided and not killed by most of the Yupa subtribes.** Incidents showing strong antagonism between snakes and humans are found throughout the narrative material. The origin story of snakes (35) explains that these reptiles are the bastard offspring of a woman and her leaf-cutter ant lover. To effect union with his human partner, the *bacháco* ant transformed himself into a snake. But in an act of jealousy, the woman's husband one day killed her paramour, thereby depriving the snake children that resulted from the ant (snake)-human union of their father.

The jealous rivalry between men and snakes seems still to exist, because in Yupa belief the killing of a snake by a pregnant woman or by her husband causes prenatal complications and miscarriages. Dreaming of jumping snakes is considered an omen of grave danger, possibly even of impending death. Hence a prudent man stays home on the day following such a dream experience rather than venture out on a hunt (20).

This same rivalry between men and snakes is also strongly expressed in the tale of a compassionate hunter who spares and raises a snake baby (34). Once it is grown up, the snake falls upon the man and devours one of his legs. Formidable flying dragons are the antagonists of men who, on their hunting expeditions, venture into the vicinity of the house of the Master of Animals. These airborne snakes pursue their unfortunate victims relentlessly until they reach and kill them. Another reason for the enmity between men and snakes is given in a fragmentary

---

*Recordings of Yupa animal calls have been published by L. T. Laffer, who released an L.P. album entitled *"Tamunangue, mosaicos del folklore Venezolano";* privately sponsored by Sonido Laffer, Caracas.
**According to Reichel-Dolmatoff (1945:54), the Yupa believe themselves to be descendants of the snake.

story (53) according to which the snakes run off with the poison that "god" had intended for men. A peculiar relationship between all kinds of snakes and the moon comes to light in another tale fragment (48) in which the house of the moon is described as being constructed of snakes tied together—posts, beams, rafters, bindings, and all.

The narratives speak of a Master of Birds (50) who devours all hunters that kill more animals than they can eat. Ruddle 1970b:59) mentions the Maracá belief that all birds have "guardians of the animals" called *yorsathë*. For instance, the type of toucan called *shatre* has a *yorsathë* who manifests himself in the form of a snake, whereas the *paujil* has a stone as guardian. Other birds also have stones, scorpions, and other things. If a man kills too many individuals of a particular species its Master will transform itself into human form and kill the offender. Apparently only solitary hunters are thus threatened, and for this reason the Yupa prefer to hunt at least in pairs; one man kills and the other is present to confuse and scare off the spirit. Among the Pariri one way of avoiding the wrath of the guardian spirit is for the hunter to leave his knife on the path to the village as an offering to appease the spirit.*

Birds in general are explained as transformed human beings of a different tribe, who were tricked into this metamorphosis by Yamore, a treacherous Yupa chief (31).

Birds of prey—buzzards, hawks, and falcons—are considered sacred by some Yupa and are not hunted. This practice finds some support in the folk literature, where the king vulture, for instance, is depicted as the creator's helper (10). Also, the giant eagle, Seremo, Master of Birds, is the eternal guardian of the mountain residence of the Master of Animals (49). Finally we must not forget to mention the woodpecker** among birds prominent in Yupa folklore, for it was he who, at the creator's command, hatched to life the first pair of human beings (1).

The Master of Animals is Peshewíipi who inhabits a rugged crag in Irapa tribal territory. He sometimes appears in the shape of a man but may also manifest himself as a frightful storm. He

---

*For further information on dreams and hunting omens among the Yupa see, Ruddle 1970b:60.
**Among the Maracá this role was played by the toad (Ruddle, personal communication).

seems to occupy a paramount position over the masters of different orders or species of the animal kingdom; for example, over Seremo, Master of Birds, and Karau, Master of Peccary (29). Karau appears as the protective Master of Animals in general and of peccary in particular. He imprisons hunters who pursue a herd of peccary and forces them to serve as swineherds. Wild boar meat is a greatly appreciated food for the Yupa, who according to tradition (42) have been hunting peccary since preagricultural times. The origin of peccary is explained as resulting from wooden disks a Yupa forefather rolled down a mountain (32, 52).

It may be that in the guise of the bush spirit Mashïramū we meet a Master of Animals figure somewhat more typical for lowland South America than the highland Master of Animals, Peshewïipi. Mashïramū has many of the features attributed to the classical prototype of the Master of Animals of Brazil and of the Amazon, Corupira or Kaapora (Zerries 1954:9). He is a powerful spirit, hostile toward mankind and deeply feared because of his aggressiveness but also and especially because his whole body is covered with thick hair and his feet are turned backward (46). Typical also for this Master of Animals is the fact that felines such as jaguars and pumas are his animal allies, so that, according to Yupa folk literature, man fought these species in order to combat Mashïramū (46).

Several customs reminiscent of Paleo-Indian hunting practices have been reported from the Yupa. So, for instance, in order to maintain or to improve his marksmanship, the hunter washes himself with certain macerated plants, or else rubs his face with specific plants to achieve hunting luck. Hunting dogs have to undergo similar preparations; they are also washed with a maceration of various plants. For the same reason several of the plants generically called *peru-kïrïkï* or *apó-kroka (apokïrïkï)* are also burned and the ashes applied to the face. The extract of a small plant called *pocha* is trickled into the eyes of the hunters and their dogs to improve their eyesight. The *pocha* juice is said also to produce a burning sensation in the intestines of the hunter and the dog, which keeps them alert for several hours (Sociedad de Ciencias Naturales La Salle 1935:345 ff.).

Monkeys, and animals in general, that fall on their backs after being shot by the hunter are left to rot (Santelos 1959–1960:

327–328). Like the pre-agricultural Sanemá and Waika, the Yupa hunter has been observed to show concern over a lost arrow and he will try to retrieve it at all costs.

FISHING

Fishing is of somewhat secondary importance to Yupa economy. Nevertheless, the Yupa do fish whenever conditions on the shallow rivers of their mountain habitat promise success. My first contact with the Yupa came about on one of the rare occasions when almost the entire Pariri subtribe had come down from their mountain villages to fish for *bagre* in the Yasa river. Their dedication was remarkable; they knew exactly how to go about their work, and all adults were familiar with the various fishing techniques. Each Yupa subtribe knows different places in their rivers where fish tend to live and feed. These places are guarded as tribal property, and they are visited each year during specific periods when they abound in fish. On these occasions the Yupa burn certain flowers and apply the ashes around their eyes to assure themselves of a good catch (Sociedad de Ciencias Naturales La Salle 1953:518).

Graveling is practiced by the women, who wade through the shallow rivers, turning over the larger stones under which the *coroncoy* might hide. The women grab the fish with their hands and kill them by biting them behind the gills. *Amarillo* is another fish caught with only the bare hands—by both women and men. This fish lives in holes in the riverbank, and is dug out with a stick or a bush knife. *Amarillo* are also killed by a bite behind the head.

A much used, but probably recent, fishing implement is the fishhook (Reichel-Dolmatoff 1945:31). Both men and women use it to catch sardines, with ants or rhinoceros beetle grubs for bait. The same bait is used for *dorado* fish. *Dientón* and *bagre* require a stronger hook and bait of sardines, while *dientón* bait is used to catch *guabina*. *Lisa* and *ekotis* are caught with small hooks and a bait of meat.

Most of these fish are also killed with the bow and arrow. This method, however, is difficult because the arrows often hit stones and the men must constantly resharpen the *macanilla* points. The Yuco tie a bunch of yellow palm fruits to a rope which they trail upstream, frightening the fish into jumping out of the water. They are then shot by the men with bows and arrows, and the women pick them up (Reichel-Dolmatoff 1945:31). Nets or fishing baskets have not been observed, and there is little use of harpoons or harpoon arrows. Weirs or dams are employed to block smaller streams (Bolinder 1925:226). The most productive method, however, is that of "poisoning" the fish. Several kinds of piscicides are used by the Venezuelan Yupa, whereas, according to Reichel-Dolmatoff (1945:31), the Colombian Yupa lack them altogether. Two species of fish poison, which the Yupa refer to as *kashi* and *wesa,* remain unidentified. *Uuha,* of which the root is used, has been identified by Sociedad de Ciencias Naturales La Salle 1953:411) as *Tephrosia singapou.* The latex of *Ceiba pentandra* has also been mentioned as a possible fish poison used by the Yupa. Women in general, especially if menstruating, must not come into contact with piscicides (Santelos 1959–1960: 43).

Only two tales of the present collection refer to fishing (22, 36). Saroro, the otter, is described as a fisherman of unusual skill who provided the entire tribe with sufficient fish to tide them over a period of scarcity (36). Fishhooks and a weir are the fishing methods employed. Mention is also made of the Master of the Fish who appears to be either identical with, or at least closely related to, the otter, as it is he who commands the fish in the rivers. In general, however, the narrative reality reflects closely the ethnographic situation, inasmuch as it attributes little importance to fishing.

DOMESTIC ANIMALS

In common with most other Indian groups, the Yupa have a tradition of capturing young wild animals and birds of which some are raised for food and others tamed as pets. In addition to this traditional use of animals, the Yupa have been recently introduced to the domestic animals of the Creoles, some of which they have adopted and integrated into both their general way of life and their system of cultivation.

Although the Yupa do tame young wild animals and birds with the objective of always keeping them as household pets, the majority eventually end up in the autosubsistence economy. The young are generally captured by men while on hunting trips. They are taken home and given to the women who raise them with affection. Bolinder (1958:148) commented that there is often lively competition among the women for the honor of raising young animals. He added that the pets are treated as members of the family and also serve to keep young children warm at night. Many women carefully prechew the young animals' food; birds especially are often fed directly from mouth to beak. Frequently an animal is even suckled at the woman's breast. Notwithstanding the bond that develops between the woman and her charge, she often has no reluctance to relinquish it to the pot when the time comes. Birds, especially in settlements located at lower altitudes, where subsistence supply is not so precarious, have a much longer survival rate as pets than do mammals.

The young of almost all of the local wild fauna may at some time be kept as pets around the homestead, but by far the most common are the various species of monkeys and birds.

Domestic animals recently adopted from the whites comprise those kept as pets, those that have become integrated into the subsistence system, and those kept to provide transportation. The most commonly encountered animals among the Yupa are the mangy dogs that flood every household. Practically speaking, these dogs are little more than pests that serve only occasionally in hunting but function mainly as scavengers and as mediocre watch-dogs. Dogs appear to have been recently introduced. Bolinder (1917:31) wrote: "Die Motilonen haben keine Haustiere; nur ausnahmsweise trifft man ein zahmes Waldhuhn oder Affen." No mention was made of the dog. In 1925, however, after having returned from his expedition to Yupa territory, he wrote: "sogar kleine Hunde hatten sie bekommen. Da die Motilonen selbst keine Haustiere haben, freuten sie sich ganz besonders darüber." According to Yupa mythology, the dog plays a vital part in guiding the dead to the next world, and to mistreat a dog would condemn its owner to wander for eternity somewhere between earth and "heaven" (6). Nevertheless, the people never seem to curry special favor with the animal to insure an easier passage to the hereafter. The only other animal pet acquired from the whites is a domestic short-haired cat.

By far the most numerous recently acquired domestic birds are the chicken, turkey, duck, and pigeon. Chickens, turkeys, and ducks are kept penned to protect them during the night (Vegamian 1951:151, 248; Hitchcock 1954:9, fig. 9). Yupa on the Apón river have been observed to use chickens for what appears to be sacrificial purposes. Bolinder (*ibid.:*135) mentioned that chickens were regarded as pets and not eaten, although the Yuco offered one to him for a meal. The same was noted for the Pariri. Other domestic animals introduced within the last thirty years include pigs, cattle, donkeys, mules, horses, sheep, and cavies. Although most families now have one or two of these domestic fowl and smaller domestic animals, only the more accessible settlements have acquired pigs, cattle, sheep, and beasts of burden. In most cases, these still play only a minor role in the Yupa way of life, although the subsistence system is gradually being adapted (notably by planting of pasture) to incorporate them.

EATING, DRINKING, AND SMOKING THE PIPE

The preparation of food is almost exclusively woman's work. Women usually accompany their men even on hunting and fishing expeditions, in order to take care of the cooking and the curing of food. Men prepare food only in exceptional cases, for example, on the warpath (14), or when the woman is away from the camp (28).

Vegetables are cooked in a pot in unsalted water. The meat of animals and fishes is roasted and birds are placed on the embers minus the head but otherwise whole. Surplus meat is smoked on a rectangular barbecue and fish may be salted down.

Salt, however, is a rare commodity among the Yupa and lemon juice mixed with ashes sometimes serves as a surrogate. Ruddle (personal communication) recorded fragments of a narrative according to which

> Salt *(inashk)* and pepper *(kakashk)* were sisters. Pepper once lived with a very small Yuco man, "because of this we take care of it today and love it."
> Pepper was taller than her sister. One day she grew tired of living in this world and asked to be killed so that she might be released. The Yuco obeyed her.
> Salt, too, used to live with the Yuco. They loved her because she was a wonderful cook and prepared tasty meals for them. Upon her sister's death she saddened, and one day she departed and went far away, never again to be seen by the Yuco.

Indeed, salt is usually lacking in Yupa kitchens, and the salty crust of roasted meat or fish is all the more appreciated. Some animal foods, such as larvae of palm beetles, and snails, are eaten raw.

Although snacks are taken whenever food is at hand, the Yupa prepare two main meals a day—at about ten in the morning and at six in the afternoon. The specter of hunger is a familiar companion of the Yupa, who normally eats as much as he can lay his hands on, rejecting food only under special circumstances, such as, for example, when he is grieving (6, 10).

Water is the main drink of these Indians but they also prepare several kinds of beverages. An unfermented drink, called *tuka,* is made from *malanga (ocumo)* roots. The women boil down batata and *malanga* roots and bury the resulting porridge in a hole in the ground. The porridge is preserved for one day in a hole lined with leaves, after which the women remove and mix it with water. *Tuka* is a tart, refreshing drink. It may also be made with ground maize and crushed sweet potatoes.

Another nonalcoholic beverage, *tami,* consists of a maceration of boiled yuca and batata in water. In a process similar to the one employed to produce *tuka,* the vegetable mash is left for a day in a basket lined with leaves and mixed with water on the following day. *Tami* is likewise enjoyed for its slightly sour flavor.

The sweet sap that collects in felled *coruba* palms is relished by the Yupa. Several days after the palm is cut, the sap changes into a lightly fermented liquid, and this, too, is consumed.

Kushara is an alcoholic beverage with more punch to it. The women boil considerable quantities of sweet potato, yuca, and bananas, crush them, and put the mash into a drinking trough filled with the juice of sugarcane. Over the next two days they place additional cooking bananas into the trough, and on the third day a rather strong fermented drink is ready for use.

A more common name for *kushara* is *chicha,* and a particularly strong *chicha* is brewed on a base of crushed maize "wrapped in leaves to make small bundles and cooked for about an hour. The maize pellets are then dried in the sun until they develop a covering of fungus through partial fermentation. The day before the feast the pellets are placed in a hollow log, the *kanoa,* together with crushed ripened bananas, yuca, and sweet potatoes. Water is poured on this mixture and fermentation commences immediately" (Métraux-Kirchoff, 1948:366).

The pygmoid Yupa have a reputation in the tribe as excellent brewers. They are also said to hold their liquor better, or at least to get drunk less often than their taller fellow tribesmen, who "during these bouts of drinking, are quick to strike and even kill other people" (16). In fact, I fear that alcoholism among the Yupa may eventually write a "firewater" ending to Yupa culture. The addiction of some groups to alcohol (and nicotine), the easy access to rum, which is liberally employed by these Indians to "improve" their *chicha,* and the generally rather low nutritional level of their food economy may already have brought these communities to a dangerous brink. This was obviously not what Oséema, the culture hero, had in mind when he introduced the forefathers of the Yupa to the brewing of *chicha* (1). And at least one story, especially its introductory explanatory motif, contains an implicit warning against drunkenness and an invitation for the Yupa rather to emulate instead the moderate drinking habits of their pygmoid fellow tribesmen who "seldom get drunk" (16).

The Yupa are avid smokers. Practically everybody smokes: men, women, and children. Young women sometimes prefer cigars but, much more typically, the Yupa smoke the pipe. They claim to have received tobacco from the Moon.

The Origin of Tobacco*

One day a Yuco was out hunting. He became completely lost and was walking in circles. Suddenly along the trail he encountered the son of the Sun. At the same moment the Sun, who was in a nest hunting *guacamayos,* spotted him. The son of the Sun took him to his father's house where he was offered a heavy dose of tobacco juice. This was in order to drug him. The Yuco refused it, for he saw the Sun wanted to kill him with an axe in order to eat him. Sun thought the Yuco was a deer.

The Moon, who had been observing the proceedings, came to Sun's house, and informed the Sun that the Yuco was not a deer but a *mushutush* (Moon's name for Yuco), and that he should not be killed. The Yuco then took an arrow to kill the Sun, but again the Moon intervened and said to the Sun, "If you kill the *mushutush* with an axe he will kill you with an arrow." The Moon then led the Yuco to his house, where he was given a meal of *batatas.* At this juncture the Moon told the Yuco that the Indian should smoke, not eat or drink, tobacco, but that the Sun and the Moon eat it.

The son of the Sun was sent to the Moon's house to fetch the Yuco because his father still wanted to eat the man. Again the Moon repeated that this being was not a deer, but a *mushutush.*

At this point the Moon told the Yuco to go home, following

*Kenneth Ruddle recorded this myth among the Maracá-Yupa of Colombia and graciously consented to let me reproduce it in the present context. Compare also narrative 42.

the indicated path, bearing to the right all the time. Before leaving, the Yuco was ordered to shoot an arrow at the Moon's house to prove to the Sun's son that the Yuco had attempted to kill the Moon. The Yuco then asked for and received tobacco seed from the Moon.

Finally, following the Moon's directions, the Yuco returned to his village, where he planted the seed.

At first the Yuco tried to smoke the leaves rolled crudely together in the form of a cigar. This was not too good, so they decided to make a container, which gradually evolved into the present-day pipe.

The Yupa grow their own tobacco and store the leaves by rolling them into packages shaped like giant cigars. The pipes are made by the men from local clay, called *wahiku*. Wahiku, goes the story (40), in mythological times used to be Tapir's companion. But while Tapir fled into the foothills, Wahiku remained with the Yupa up in the mountains. Tobacco pipes are certainly of considerable antiquity among American Indians, but the type made and used by the Yupa seems to show some European influence. The fired clay bowl is of a fine grade and is decorated with incised patterns of lines and dots. The wooden stem may taper into a wide and flat mouthpiece. Some craftsmen decorate their pipe-stems by winding cotton thread of different colors around them.

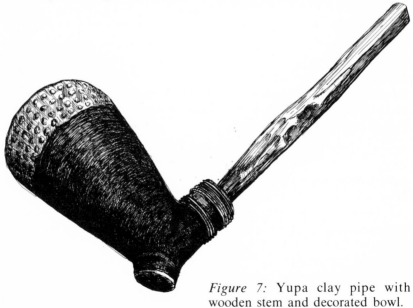

Figure 7: Yupa clay pipe with wooden stem and decorated bowl.

It was the Moon, then, who advised the Yupa to smoke tobacco rather than to imbibe it, the latter practice being reserved to the Sun and the Moon. It would seem that the Yupa obeyed this stricture, since cigar and pipe smoking are the most common ways in which tobacco is used by these Indians.

Considering this, it came as something of a surprise to learn from one narrative (21) that a woman, taking care of her sick brother, one day "set out to make *pamocha.* She burned a quantity of stalks of the royal palm, sieved water through the ashes, and then boiled down the liquid. She gave her old brother the salt that had remained on a roll of tobacco to chew for a quid. The sick man was very happy over this special labor of love and chewed away the whole day."

To my knowledge there is thus far no ethnographic information concerning the practice of tobacco chewing among the Yupa. As described in the narrative, the method of producing the quid by the woman is reminiscent of similar practices among the Cariban tribes of the Lesser Antilles and the Guyanas; for example, Pemon, Acawaio, Patamona. The Goajiro and the Chibcha, neighbors of the Yupa, chew a tobacco paste, instead of a quid of the Yupa type, which rather resembles that of the Yanoama. The *pamocho* quid of the Yupa narrative, then, represents unexpected evidence for a tradition of tobacco chewing in northwestern South America.

The Yupa pipe looks rather foreign and, curiously, so does the Yupa word for it, *kachimbo.* But even for the tobacco itself the Yupa do not employ a Cariban term: they call it *tápak,* while *pamocho* refers to the salty ashes (*pãmo* = salt) rather than to the tobacco leaves themselves. What all this adds up to, I believe, is that the use of tobacco in its present form may not be completely autochthonous among the Yupa.

The etiological story notwithstanding, tobacco drinking or the consumption of the plant in any form has never acquired ritual significance among them. On the contrary, in keeping with the etymological evidence, plus the fact that smoking of tobacco is indulged in by everybody irrespective of age and sex, points to a generalized secular use of tobacco among these Indians.

The Society

FAMILY AND KINSHIP

The nuclear family is a well-established functioning socioeconomic unit within tribal society. Most of the activities of the daily routine develop primarily among the members of this smallest social unit of these Indians, which from an economical point of view is almost wholly self-sufficient.

As a rule, each nuclear family owns a house, and only in rare occasions have several such families been observed sharing the same roof. In polygamous families the husband sleeps between his wives, and children spread their sleeping mat close to that of their mother. Residence is initially uxorilocal but becomes neolocal after one or two years of marriage.

Authority within the nuclear family is patripotestal although the husband frequently consults with his spouse or spouses before making any decisions. Consanguineal and affinal kin ties have been observed to be strong bonds of solidarity among the Yupa. Children were found to obey both parents equally well. In polygamous families the wife married first outranks her co-wives.

Preliminary data on the kinship system (of the Pariri) indicate that they practice a bifurcate merging system of the Iroquois type; cross-cousins are terminologically differentiated from parallel-cousins who, in turn, are treated like classificatory siblings. Cross-cousin marriage is permitted, and the conflict described in narrative 17 is generated precisely because the hero of the story commits incest by marrying his parallel-cousin. Ego may also marry the niece/nephew of his sibling of opposite sex. Kin terms are commonly employed in day-to-day relations, but personal names are also used (Wilbert 1962a:115–120).

CHIEFS AND SHAMANS

The various Yupa subtribes are independent endogamous bands consisting of a number of extended families with nuclear family households. They enjoy political autonomy and live in almost perpetual hostility toward one another. Each subtribe recognizes a chief or headman.

The Yupa recognize two different kinds of shaman, the *tomaira* and the *tuano*. Every local group among the Pariri has its own *tomaira*, the religious leader of the tribe, who functions as intermediary between his people and the supernatural. He stipulates when and how ceremonials are to be held, what preparations are necessary, what songs shall be sung, what dances danced.

Although any male Yupa can theoretically become a *tomaira*, only one who experiences a special calling will eventually assume the office. His vocation manifests itself in his dreams: specifically, he hears a song while he sleeps and on awakening is able to reproduce it exactly. If the song thus sung is original (i.e., a true sign of a supernatural dream experience), rather than a reproduction of one he has heard his *tomaira* sing, then the village *tomaira* will mark him as a potential candidate for the office. From time to time the candidates engage in a song contest where they can demonstrate the extent of their repertoire. A serious candidate will have "captured" a number of songs in his dreams, and for each such song (called *homáikĩ*) mastered perfectly he will mark a symbol in black (or red or blue) on a wooden tablet *(wĩsĩyákepu)*. The leading *tomaira* will often have as many as sixty songs at his command. For life crises (birth, naming, marriage, and burial ceremonies) and harvest festivals specific songs are chosen by the *tomaira* from his store, and the particular mnemonic symbol for each is copied onto a smaller wooden block *(tio-tio)*. He then sets about rehearsing his villagers in singing the designated songs and learning the dance that belongs to each. In the birth ceremony, for example, the *tomaira* sets his *tio-tio* on the ground in front of him, seats the new mother and her infant by his side, and, recalling the song designated by the mark on his *tio-tio*, leads the villagers in song and dance from his commanding spot in the center of the village plaza.

The Irapa celebrate a harvest festival of thanksgiving not unlike that of the Pariri. On the morning of the festival the *tomaira* sends several men into the fields to harvest the maize in baskets. The stalks are carefully cut up and stacked in small mounds, while the ears of maize are taken to the wife of the *tomaira*, who makes from them one large cake and three small ones for each of the participants in the ceremony. These are laid upon a huge green leaf inside the house. As soon as the cakes are ready the dance begins. Men and women take their positions. Each of the men carries a small bundle of corncobs on his back, to which the women hold on with one hand as they dance the round dance and sing to the accompaniment of small flutes played by the men. The dance ends toward midday when the *tomaira* steps into the home and lets a woman offer him a piece of meat. He tastes it before eating the large maize cake in the silent presence of the others. Then he distributes three of the small cakes to each participant. After all have eaten, the dancing continues until evening—without benefit of intoxicating beverages. The only drink permitted is a sweet, nonalcoholic infusion made of maize. The evening sees the distribution by the *tomaira* of the entire harvest of maize among all the families in the village. This is the festival in honor of Oséema, who originally blessed the Yupa with maize and who determines the size of each harvest.

The *tuano* is a shaman with very different functions. He is a herbalist or medicine man. The office demands long and arduous preparation for mastery of medicinal plant knowledge, the art of diagnosing, and the curing of illnesses. The *tuano*, as well as his wife, the *tuana*,* knows which plants, which barks, which leaves, which roots, must be gathered, and how they should be prepared. He is expert at diagnosis—of the illness itself, of the appropriate herbal medicine, and whether it is to be taken internally, applied to the skin, or used as a bath. It is true that all Yupa adhere to established protective measures against malevolent spirits and are acquainted with the curative properties of various plants; but it is their *tuano* who possesses—over and above superb familiarity with botanical remedies—the ability to turn the magical potential of each substance to his own use. Thus the *tuano* is set apart from other men through his skill and through his metaphysical connections. The same holds for his wife, and for these reasons it is the *tuana* in each village who often gives pubescent girls their formal instruction during the time of their first menstrual seclusion.

The narrative reality parallels quite closely and supplements our ethnographic data on the *tuano*. In contrast, the *tomaira* plays no role whatever in the oral literature.

The first time the narratives describe a *tuano* shaman in action (3) he appears in the form of the cayman. As his likely prototype, the cayman of the floodplains of the Amazon basin, the shaman-

---

*The hispanicized form *tuana* is my own.

cayman dominates the scene of a primordial flood, "a gigantic sheet of water bordered all about by a wall of mud." Cayman was the only one who could dive deep enough to dig at the wall from below until the water broke through. The cayman-shaman, like a diving god of the Underworld, directed the rescue of the sole survivors of the great deluge.

The human *tuano* and his wife are introduced in oral literature as herbalists who not only know the right plant to counteract a poisoning he has suffered, but who also have knowledge of certain herbs the sap of which, when sprinkled on the paths to their village, can intercept aggressive evil spirits of the night. Better yet, the *tuano* shaman and his wife are capable of destroying the entire population of their enemies, the Meteru, by means of mannikins made of human bones and covered with beeswax.*

In another story (15) we see the *tuano* and his wife as the only humans resistant enough to survive the onslaught of an evil spirit who exterminated mankind with the common cold. They found an herb whose juice, when squeezed into the river system, purified the polluted waters of the entire country. Like the first couple of human beings, they repopulated the world and established the traditional moral code of Yupa culture.

Then, to avert a famine caused by violation of the incest taboo, the *tuano*-shaman embarked on a celestial journey. Lifted by the power of contemplation and prayer the shaman beseeched the sun to continue taking its daily course around the earth, dispel the clouds whose rain had flooded the earth, and restore the fertility of the eroded fields of the Indians (15).

Thus the *tuano*-shaman is capable of descent to the nadir of the Underworld and of ascent to the zenith of the celestial dome. His shamanic power is grounded in his pharmaceutical knowledge and in the strength of his meditation. He upholds the society's moral strength and makes his fellowmen invulnerable in times of war (17). Mankind would long since have perished several times over had it not been for the shamanic knowledge and power of the *tuano*.

---

*Compare the *tuano*'s power of creating life from mannikins with that of the creator of the first narrative.

The Life Cycle

CONCEPTION AND PREGNANCY

The Yupa are fully aware that pregnancy results from sexual intercourse. To promote conception the husband brews a concoction from the sap of various leaves which both he and his wife drink. Contraception is also practiced, with the wife chewing a piece of *sukuhta* creeper.

The Yupa believe that the fetus grows from the male semen and the woman's blood. For the nine to ten lunar months of pregnancy the expectant parents observe a number of food taboos: the flesh of anteater and sloth (to prevent miscarriage); the flesh of tapir, cayman, nutria (lest the father die); the flesh of the toucan (lest the child be cross-eyed); crabs (lest the child wail unbearably during his first year of life); the flesh of the *honambru* fish (lest the child suffer severe nosebleeds); the flesh of the *bagre* fish (lest the child suffer ulcers of the tongue); honey (lest the baby's skull be soft). Should the parents kill a snake during the pregnancy period, they may count on sickness and eventual death for their offspring.*

The narratives contain almost no data on what one would consider "normal aspects" of human reproduction. Several unusual conceptions occur; for example, a woman becomes pregnant through intercourse with an artificial phallus (10), while her daughter conceives a boy child from the sea (10). Rapes (4, 44) and seductions (17, 24, 25) also occur.

BIRTH AND INFANCY

With the onset of serious labor pains the woman retreats to a hut in the forest, accompanied by two experienced female relatives. The birth hut has been purposely erected at some distance from the village lest the inhabitants be supernaturally jeopardized in the event of a stillbirth. To accelerate her labor the woman is given a brew made from water mixed with the powdered seed of the *ojo de zamuro*. Supported from behind, the woman gives birth in a squatting position, the cord is cut some distance from

*See discussion on snakes and sexual antagonism pp. 35–38.

the navel by the sharp-edged leaf of the *bijaio,* and the afterbirth is placed intact in a basket and hung on a tree (among the Pariri) or buried immediately outside the hut. Mother and child are washed repeatedly with heated water before returning to their home in the village. The mother rests for a few days before returning to her normal household tasks, during which period she consumes four leaves of the *maratei* plant each day. The umbilical cord dries up and is placed into the open fire. The baby is quickly passed over the flames as a purification.

Apparently there is no *couvade* for the father, but he is barred from attending the birth of his child. While mother and child rest at home, he leaves for a special hunt. He will offer her the results of his hunt, which she is obliged to refuse; the next day, however she will accept his catch.

The first social ceremony for the new Yupa occurs two or three weeks after birth. Ruddle (1970) reports on the ceremony as observed among the Maracá on the birth of a baby. To ensure the offspring's future courage and prowess as a hunter, the father goes alone into the forest to search out the nests of wasps and bees for their larvae, braving their stings without benefit of fire and smoke. Meanwhile the mother prepares a great quantity of *chicha,* and a little wrap of *caña brava* sticks "two hands plus one little finger" long is fashioned for the child to wear at the dance. The father gathers a large number of *sahpatirah* plants, three for each male participating in the ceremony. In front of the homes a line of holes has been dug in the ground into each of which is set one plant. The dance commences with the child cloaked in his *caña brava* wrap on the back of his father. Each man dances with the child on his back during which time he must destroy three of the plants with five arrows. When the leaves have been shot off all the plants the dance ends and the feast of the roasted larvae and *chicha* begins.

Among the Pariri the birth ceremony is directed by the *tomaira,* the village priest-shaman. The mother prepares a roasted hen or other large bird and a quantity of *kusare.* Half is for the headman of the village; the other half is offered to the *tomaira* by the father, accompanied by two men and three women. Ascertaining that there will be sufficient food and drink for the number of anticipated participants, the *tomaira* sets a date for the ceremony two or three weeks hence. On the appointed day the parents, accompanied by the local group and relatives from distant vaillages, arrive with the baby at the home of the *tomaira*. Formalized dancing and singing led by the *tomaira* commence, the ceremony stretching on for two or three days, ending only when the supply of food and drink is exhausted.

Santelos (1959–1960:303) reports that a special ceremony takes place sometime following the birth of a male child into an Irapa village. Over a slow fire the Indians roast a number of *kasha*, a species of wasp known for its fiery and painful sting. The resultant black ash is given to the *tuano*-shaman of the village, who presses some onto his thumb and rubs it on the baby's forehead and chin, right under the lower lip. The purpose of this rite is to ensure that the boy will grow up to become as fierce and aggressive as the *kasha* wasp, and that he will rise to the defense of his people as does a shaman.

Although the new Yupa has left her womb, the infant is constantly with his mother, the breast his constant solace. If he is not cradled in her arms he rides with her everywhere in a sling of thick woven straps passed over her shoulder or forehead.

At four months of age the infant is the object of a second rite, the naming ceremony, which functions as his official presentation to, and acceptance into, the group. The *tomaira* gives the baby his first solid food (banana pap) and assigns to him a personal name, usually the diminutive of a bird or plant designation. This name is held secret, for to speak it aloud would expose the individual to the malevolent influence of an evil shaman. Should the baby be offered solid food before receiving it at the hands of the *tomaira*, he would remain forever "nameless" and hence expose himself and his family to danger.

CHILDHOOD

Children grow up in the house of their parents (or occasionally of their grandparents), running free and naked, to the age of two or three, sleeping, eating, and performing whatever economic duties they can in an atmosphere of warmth and affection. Without recourse to physical punishment the parents manage the effective socialization of the child through affection and the occasional threat of supernatural retaliation for deviant behavior. Thus the young Yupa learns to control his aggression against his peers, to share his material blessings with others, and above all to limit his excursions to the bounds of the village.

For children there are games like cat's cradle, archery, and making music with instruments fashioned from wood and shells of fruit, but just as adult labors are divided according to sex, so also is the play of the children sexually differentiated. The three-year-old boy has his own little bow and arrow and eventually will accompany his father on hunting expeditions. The little girl learns from her mother and gradually becomes familiar with such household duties (cooking, weaving, washing, collecting) as are considered the province of the woman. Her formal instruction is completed when she goes into seclusion upon her first menstruation.

Birth and infancy receive scarcely any attention in the collected folktales, except in cases where women bring forth abnormal offspring as a result of irregular unions; for example, a woman gives birth to snakes (35); a man fathers palms (25); a bitch has offspring with human bodies but dogs' heads as a result of bestiality (27); and the children of pygmoid mother and a Yupa father are of small stature like their mother but have a digestive tract like their father.

Children likewise receive little mention in the narrative material. We hear of one father who devours his children (42); children are described as close enough to their real father so as to recognize an impostor (45); or the gradual transformation of their father's baby (37). We hear of a mother's love for her daughter, whom she nurtures, in the face of public criticism, as she is transforming into a deer (33). But stepchildren do not always fare that well (36, 41). Other than that the narrative reality contains practically nothing that would supplement our ethnographic knowledge of Yupa infancy and children.

PUBERTY AND ADOLESCENCE

A girl's first menstruation signals her physical readiness to pass from childhood to adulthood. On the day of her first menstruation, at age twelve or thirteen, she is accompanied by her mother or sister to a specially constructed hut in the woods. Her seclusion for three weeks or so allows for her ritual formal instruction and insures the metaphysical safety of the village through her physical removal for the time of menstrual bleeding. The child must abstain from all meat and vegetable food except for maize, birds, and water. Her hair is shorn; her nails are cut; her feet tread on specially placed stones to the place of defecation. These and the food taboos are protective measures to protect the candidate from evil spirits and to prevent her blood from coagulating. Her food is prepared by the female attendant; she sits facing away from the entrance on a bed of leaves, and every morning is visited by the wife of a *tuano* of her village for ritual instruction in the rights and duties of a Yupa woman. At the end of her isolation she is allowed to cook a meal for herself and her companion after which the cooking pot is smashed on a stone. Then she mashes a large plantain and, mixing it with a little water, makes a paste which she smears on a rock (to protect her family from evil spirits). Now she can return to the village—an adult woman, a knowledgable woman, a marriageable woman.

There is no specific rite of passage known for boys of corresponding age. But when his physical maturation is complete the young Yupa will be wholly conversant in the duties and responsibilities of an adult male.

Apparently, adolescent boys and girls indulge in a certain amount of sexual activity—opportunity for which occurs at the numerous festivals held throughout the year.

There is somewhat more descriptive mention of adolescence in Yupa folk literature than there is of infancy and childhood. The culture hero, Oséema, appears on earth as a single, adolescent boy who enchants the women (41). The dangers to which an adolescent girl is exposed during her first menstruation are described in a short narrative (44). In one of the myths (6), there is depicted a most lyrical scene of tender love between adolescents, which on the other hand, also tells of the fierceness of adolescent jealousy and rivalry that—at least according to the narrative reality—young lovers are up against. Some unusual lovers are also mentioned in the corpus of narrative; an ant-lover in male form (35), an anteater paramour (28), and a rainbow abductor (4).

MARRIAGE AND ADULTHOOD

Marriage comes early to the Yupa, as a result of either a pre-arranged betrothal, a personal decision, or an abduction. Cross-cousin marriage is preferred and sought within the subtribe. Abduction is in contravention of the latter preference; the woman is carried off by her captor to become his wife but seldom, if ever, is wholly accepted by her new group.

Usually a girl marries a young man in another local group, to whom her father has betrothed her as a child. While she sits isolated in the menstruation hut, the prospective groom presents himself to her parents with gifts of game, other foodstuffs, and clothing. He is desirous of a beautiful bride with firm, upright breasts and sturdy legs, a young woman skilled in the domestic arts, industrious, and faithful. She, being of a more practical turn of mind, dreams of a good provider. Negotiations proceed, and an understanding among parents, daughter, and suitor having been reached, a date for the marriage ceremony is fixed. If it is revealed, however, that in the meantime the girl has had a relationship with another man, the decision goes against the first applicant.

All local groups of the subtribe are invited to the wedding feast to sing, dance, eat, and drink. The bridegroom (but not his bride) may drink as much as he wishes, but dancing is forbidden to both as they sit alone in the central plaza while the guests dance and sing around them. The celebration lasts for several days and nights until the supply of food and drink is exhausted, at which point the guests wend their way homeward.

A man without the wherewithal to provide for such a materially burdensome wedding celebration will live with a girl without benefit of ceremony until she eventually marries. Children resulting from such a union, however, belong solely to the woman and therefore little regard is held for an unrecognized relationship. Thus a man will work and plan for the day when he can marry properly.

But to marry is not to live happily ever after. Well aware that he must be absent from the village for long periods of time, the Yupa husband is consumed by almost paranoid jealousy over his woman, who is the object of many a covetous look. Bitter quarreling and fights to the death arise from such unavoidable situations. Marital infidelity sometimes gives the aggrieved husband the right to material compensation from the girl's father. More frequently the cuckolded husband challenges his wife's seducer to a ritual duel. It is the traditional duty of the woman's brothers and brothers-in-law to carry out the duel against an equal number of friends of the seducer. The husband himself is allowed to participate only if it can be demonstrated that his prior conduct toward his wife was wholly exemplary.

The warriors on both sides line up facing one another. Armed with a heavy bow, each in turn strikes as hard a blow as he can to the head of his opponent—turn and turnabout, blow for blow, until but one man is left standing. The duel becomes chiefly a matter of pride in demonstrating the superiority of one local group over another, for its outcome has little to do with the future course of the marriage. Even if her husband's team is victorious, the woman may choose to leave her man and village for that of her seducer.

If a man wishes to divorce his wife, he simply leaves her. She keeps the children and has not long to wait for a new husband. One has the impression that Yupa marriages are not particularly stable.

First marriages usually result in uxorilocal residence for a few years, during which time the husband is expected to perform bride service, such as hunting game for his wife's parents and clearing new fields.

A second marriage is contracted like the first, except that there is no marriage festival, and there is little, if any, bride service. Polygamy, though permitted, is scarcely realistic in Yupa society. But when it does occur the first wife holds authority over the second, although each sleeps in a separate section of the house.

It would seem that the Yupa of both sexes spend the bulk of the daylight hours on activities related to the quest of food. Nevertheless, there is time after the main meal to sit around the fire as night falls. Visitors come to joke, tell stories, and to sing before returning to their own houses.

The Yupa life cycle is punctuated throughout the year by various ceremonies and festivities, during which time the daily routine for all is suspended. The local groups gather for the formal celebration, singing, dancing, feasting and drinking the enormous quantities of *chicha* which, together with the lifting of the usual rigid sexual controls, provide periodic release of built-up tensions. The actual *dramatis personae* of the narratives are mainly adults, and here the narrative reality contains some information on adult roles. Women may be given into marriage for political reasons against their will (17), and cooperate with their husbands (41). They stand with them in times of trial, even in the face of conjugal infidelity

(9) and public ridicule (30). Polygamy is mentioned on various occasions as a licit form of marriage (11, 30, 45), cross-cousin marriage is permitted (17), and loving husbands are expected to provide for their wives (25). Irregular marriages occur also as unions of man to animals (27), trees (25), and subterranean dwarfs (8). The incest taboo, which includes mothers (41), mothers-in-law (24), siblings (1, 18, 41) and parallel cousins (17), is variously referred to. Transgressions of the taboo are severely punished (15, 24). In fact, in one case mankind is nearly completely wiped out (3); in another a war between two tribal groups ensues as a consequence of a forced parallel-cousin marriage involving the death of the woman through mental cruelty and humiliation (17).

Sisters are supposed to care for their widowed brothers (21), and young couples for their parents-in-law (19, 24). People revenge the murder of their kin (11, 21). Hospitality is valued highly (6, 19, 41), including sexual hospitality (7, 41), and slander has dire consequences (18). Ridicule calls for drastic measures (11, 30).

Some information is given in the narratives concerning the prevailing division of labor. Men do the hunting and pursue the animals either singly (30) or in groups; for example, a father with his sons (7) or several men together (14, 29, 41, 42). They hunt by day and by night (41). Unsuccessful hunters are ridiculed and may prefer self-mutilation and suicide to sustaining humiliation through public mockery (30).

SICKNESS AND DEATH

The messenger of death is sickness, the cause of which is rooted in the supernatural realm. Most afflictions, however, can be cured by wholly natural ways and means. And therein lies the difference between the Yupa and other tribes of Venezuelan Indians for whom one is accustomed to finding cures for magically induced illness solely by magical means. Not so with the Yupa, whose *tuano* seeks to heal with pharmaceutical therapy even maladies induced by spirits. The most common illnesses are diseases of the respiratory tract and of the digestive system. Venereal diseases are seldom seen, being limited to contact zones on the border regions of the Indians' territory. More frequent are cases of yaws and goiter.

At the moment of death the soul forsakes the body through the right hand. The voices of friends and relatives rise in wailing and mourning as the corpse is wrapped in mats and set upon a platform amid the sheltering branches of a tree. Months later secondary burial takes place in which, traditionally, the bones are carefully packed into a bundle and borne to the tribal ossary—a cave in the mountains. Nowadays, however, an earthly grave is the last resting place for the secondary burial. The house of the deceased is burned to the ground, his belongings broken. His wife cuts her hair, restricts her diet to but a few permitted (unseasoned!) foods, and withdraws from society for a prescribed period of time. The death ceremony is the same for all, male or female.

The introdution to one myth (8) reads: "When a Yupa dies, all his friends and kin come together to talk about him to reminisce, to weep and to wail." It also mentions the ossary used by the Yupa as a depository for the bone bundles of secondary burial, and drinking feasts that are given in connection with funerary rites (21).

Scourges such as the common cold of the white man, which swept the country like an apocalyptic horseman, are personified causes of sickness (15). But epidemics can also be sent by sorcery and by means of magic figurines (9).

Certain death can be prevented according to one tale (20) by heeding dreams involving flutes of the dead, jumping snakes, red batata, red stones, or night spirits, known as Karau. Violent deaths occur in narrative reality in the form of suicides (6, 30), homicides (6, 9 [intended], 11, 21, 40) or casualties of warfare (14). Other deaths occur when people are swallowed by the earth (12, 13, 18), or die of shame (17, 19, 28) or by accident (22, 42). Whenever possible homicide is not committed in open confrontation. The murderer prefers to catch the victim off guard (11, 13, 21, 35, 40, 47). The possessions of the dead are destroyed (18), and proper funeral is refused to a stingy person (19).

Plate 1. Yupa houses are often situated on mountain tops.

Plate 2. View of the interior of a Yupa house.

Plate 3. Macoita Chief and his family.

Plate 4. Making fire with drill.

Plate 5. Children carrying water.

Plate 6. Hut with woman and child.

Plate 7. Woman beating cotton on mat to remove seeds and impurities.

Plate 8. Woman weaving on robe.

Plate 9. Playing axe flute.

Plate 10. Indians drinking chicha from "kanoa."

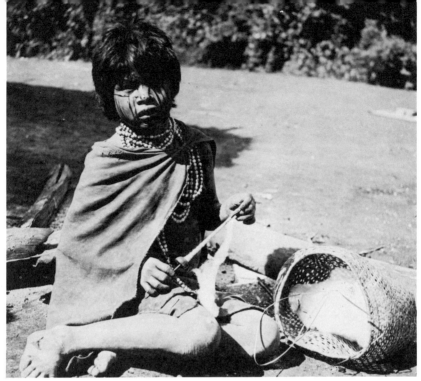

Plate 11. Young girl spinning cotton thread.

Plate 13. Preparing a meal of sweet yuca.

Plate 12. Hunter with bow and arrows, bamboo quiver with small bow and arrows.

Plate 14. Pygmoid man during a drinking spree.

Plate 15. Woman plaiting a straw sleeping mat.

Plate 16. Pygmoid men enjoying their pipes.

Plate 17. Pygmoid man applying facial paint.

Plate 18. Young woman applying facial paint.

Plate 19. Woman mealing corn for chicha.

II: Narrative Material
and Motif Content

The Folktales

1. THE CREATION OF THE FIRST HUMAN BEINGS

One day God betook himself into the forest, where he went about striking different trees with his axe. He passed from one tree to another until he found one which spurted blood the moment the blade fell upon it. He felled this tree and from its wood he carved two figures—two little human children. Thereupon he felled a second tree, made a box from the trunk, and laid the two figures in this box. Then, calling a bird, the woodpecker, he commanded it to sit down upon the figures, closed the box with a cover, and left it in the forest.

Several days later the companion of God went into the forest and was greatly astonished suddenly to hear voices. Following the direction of the sounds she discovered the box and ever so carefully raised the cover. To her great surprise she found two little, live human children inside and the bird as well. She took the children home with her and reared them until they were full-grown and could take each other as man and wife. Many children, born to this young pair of human beings, eventually married one another, so that after a few years there was a great number of people upon the earth.

One day God mingled with the humans, calling them to gather before him. He told them how they had sprung from the figures of wood, and how, therefore, they were all the descendants of one original pair of siblings. Since there was now a sufficient number of people on the earth, it was commanded that henceforth no man might take his sister as his wife.

The people agreed and promised to keep this law. Then God introduced the woodpecker bird to the Yupa as his helper in the work of giving them the form of living human beings.

On the last day of his stay among the Yupa, God arranged a great festival at which time he taught them the art of brewing *chicha*. Finally, before taking leave of them, he promised that after this life he would call all Yupa to join him in his land.

Summary: *The Creation of the First Human Beings*

God makes two human children from a tree. They eventually

marry, and their children in turn. Finally God forbids marriage between brothers and sisters, and promises the Yupa a life after death in his land.

Motif Content: *The Creation of the First Human Beings*

A32.3.	Creator's wife.
A141.1.+.	God makes wooden images and vivifies them. (A141.1. God makes automata and vivifies them.)
A545.	Culture hero establishes customs.
A1252.	Creation of man from wood.
A1252.1.	Mankind from vivified wooden image.
A1271.	Origin of first parents.
A1273.1.	Incestuous first parents.
A1426.2.1.	Introduction of brewing.
A1552.1.	Why brothers and sisters do not marry.
A1552.3.	Brother-sister marriage of children of first parents.
B461.1.	Helpful woodpecker.
F811.20.	Bleeding tree.
V311.	Belief in the life to come.

2. DAY AND NIGHT

In the beginning of time there were two suns, one of which went up when the other went down.

One day Kopecho* invited one of the suns to a festival. So he went there to take part, but not, however, to dance.

Kopecho had made a great fire and danced to and fro before it in an enticing manner. Finding himself very attracted to the dancing woman, Sun rose and went toward her. He had not noticed, however, that behind the fire lay a deep pit with glowing coals into which he fell before he ever reached Kopecho.

But Sun, being quite used to heat, did not burn. He climbed out of the pit, seized the seductive woman by the hips, and tossed her into the water. Kopecho was transformed into a frog, and since that day she has lived in the water. Sun's body, however, became white and his eyes turned to glowing coals. He returned

---

*The reader will note that Kopecho is feminine in this tale and masculine in story 6, in accordance with the genders assigned by my informant.

to the firmament and became the moon. Thus began night and day.

Sun and Moon are brothers,* who cannot get along with each other. The stars, who belong to the people of Sun, have no liking for the moon, for once he, the moon, refused to give a star one of his many daughters. Every month they fall upon the moon to beat him. The moon stoops down then and gets very small.

The son of the moon is also a star, but he cannot be seen. The many daughters of Moon and his wife likewise cannot be seen, for they always stay at home. The Milky Way is the track of Sun and Moon.

Summary: *Day and Night*

Long ago there were two suns. Through a woman's trick one becomes the moon. The stars and the sun dislike the moon; they beat him every month and he becomes very small. His wife, daughter, and son are invisible.

Motif Content:	*Day and Night*
A711.3.+.	Originally two suns but no moon (A711.3. Originally a moon but no sun.)
A736.3.	Sun and moon as brothers.
A736.3.3.	Sun and his brother rise and set alternately.
A740.	Creation of the moon.
A745.	Family of the moon.
A755.6.	Moon's phases as punishment for moon's misdoing.
A759.3.	Why the moon is pale.
A764.1.+.	Moon's son is a star. (A764.1. Stars as children of the moon.)
A778.	Origin of the Milky Way.
A1068.+.	Sun thrown on fire. (A1068. Sun thrown on fire: period of darkness, rain.)
A1170.	Origin of night and day.
D195.+.	Transformation: woman to frog. (D195. Transformation: man to frog.)
Q551.3.2.3.	Punishment: transformation into frog.

---

*For more information on these celestial brothers see: narratives 7 and 42. For their position in a wider ethnological context see: Gusinde 1930.

3. THE FLOOD

A long time ago a great flood arose, from which only twenty pairs of human beings and a few animals were able to save themselves on top of a high mountain. One day a Yupa declared that he was truly the bird woodpecker, and would fly off to ascertain the extent of the flood. He found out that it was a gigantic sheet of water bordered all about by a wall of mud. Now the cayman wanted to determine the depth of the water. So he threw in a big wild boar first, and then a tapir, and then all the other animals one after the other—all of which drowned without exception, so deep was the water. Finally the crab decided to dive in; four days and four nights passed before he came up again. Now the cayman was a *tuano* (medicine man) who could dive that deeply without danger. He ordered the turtle and the armadillo to swim with him to the sand wall. Once there he dove under the water with the turtle to dig at the wall from below. The armadillo meanwhile was to work from above. Soon the wall gave way, and the water broke through. A good deal of sand remained lying on the backs of the armadillo, the turtle, and the cayman. Even today one can still see sand on their backs.

Summary: *The Flood*

During a flood the cayman, the turtle, and the armadillo break the sand wall bordering the water. To this day they still have sand on their backs.

Motif Content:	*The Flood*
A812.	Earth diver.
A1009.+.	Flood. (A1009. World catastrophes—misc.)
A1022.	Escape from deluge on mountain.
A2291.+.	Animal characteristics acquired during flood. (A2291. Animal characteristics obtained during deluge.)

4. THE RAINBOW

A woman once went to the river to fetch water when suddenly Rainbow appeared. He wanted the woman for his own and carried her up to the sky. But the closer the woman came to the top of the sky, the more she was scorched until finally she was all burned up and fell back to earth.

The other women of the tribe missed their companion and ran to the river to look for her. But all they found were her charred remains lying on the bank.

Motif Content: *The Rainbow*
D2121.5.+. Magic journey: woman carried to sky by rainbow. (D2121.5. Magic journey: man carried by spirit or devil.)
R39.+. Abduction by rainbow. (R39. Abduction—misc.)

5. THE ORIGIN OF FIRE

In the beginning the Yupa had no fire. One day a man went into the woods and stumbled over two stones lying by a cotton bush. Bending over and picking them up in his hand, he studied these stones for a while, and then threw them carelessly to one side as he wished to continue his way. Suddenly he saw a strange man standing opposite him. The stranger introduced himself as the owner of the stones and asked the Yupa why he had not taken the stones with him since it was the first time he had ever seen such. The Yupa replied that he had not the faintest idea what to do with them. At this the stranger laughed. "These are no ordinary stones," he explained. "These are firestones— *wéhra-támi.*" With this he struck the stones together and showed the astonished man how one may catch the leaping spark in the cotton. Then he gave him the stones and bade him take them home (for in the mountains there were more of them). He should, however, take the utmost care neither to let the firestones fall into the hands of menstruating women nor let the latter handle the fire from the stones—lest all fall sick. With this the stranger vanished—he was the Lord of Fire—and from that day on the Yupa possessed fire.

Summary: *The Origin of Fire*
The Lord of Fire teaches a Yupa man how to make fire with two stones.

Motif Content:	*The Origin of Fire*
A1414.4.	Origin of fire—gift from god.
A1414.5.	Origin of flint and tinder.
C145.+.	Tabu: not to touch firestones during menses. (C145. Tabu: not to touch certain things during menses.)
H976.	Task performed by mysterious stranger.

6. THE LAND OF THE DEAD

Once during a festival a young man fell in love with a girl of his tribe. This love she returned and allowed him to lead her into the forest. Hearing of this and full of envy, the other men of the tribe looked with jealous eyes upon the young man, shot him in the forest at the very first chance, and buried him on the spot.

The girl was so grieved over the death of her lover that she would not leave his grave the whole week long no matter how hard they tried to take her away. She remained sitting at the grave, crying bitterly, eating nothing.

She had mourned one whole week when one night the dead

Figure 8: Strawhats made by the men betray European influence.

lover appeared to her. Why did she grieve so long for him? So she told him of her great love, a love too strong for death to alter. Upon hearing this the dead one ordered her to make a little *támi* so that together they might take a long journey. Immediately the girl began to make a little supply of *támi* and went to the place where her dead loved one had promised to meet her. There they found each other. Her lover, however, did not appear in human form, but rather as cloud and wind. He encouraged her to set forth; she could feel him following her like a gentle breeze.

First the path led through a thick forest. Finally it brought them to the house of Kopecho, the Lord of Frogs. Kopecho gave them this order: each must make a piece of basketry. The young man made a hat with feathers on it *(pesówa)* and the girl made a basket *(menure)*. They were given the reeds by Kopecho, who examined the finished pieces with close attention. He was pleased with the hat of the man, but found the basket of the girl poorly made. Then Kopecho led both of them behind the house where two paths began. He sent the girl down one path and the man down the other. Perhaps, she said, they might meet again a day's journey hence.

The girl went along the path and was soon attacked by all sorts of wild beasts. They jumped at her seeking to devour her, yet at the last instant, frightened, they always backed off. Finally the girl came to a river, on which there rolled a huge, hollow, tree trunk reaching from shore to shore. The path led through this log. When she first set foot in it she was terrified by the screaming people who tumbled about inside striving vainly to find a way out. All of them tried to cling to her, but could not hold her fast. Finally she reached the end of the tree trunk and could happily step out of it. Once outside she met no more wild beasts and the cries of the tumbling people could be heard no longer.

A little further on both paths came together. Both had started at the house of Kopecho, and now went in the same direction. At the fork of the road the girl met her lover who was happy to see her again, for he knew that she had traveled the Path of Unworthy People. (Kopecho recognizes the unworthy people by the fact that they cannot properly finish the basketry work which he orders them to make. So he sends them along the path of the unrighteous. Either they are devoured by the wild beasts along the way, or those who do reach the spinning tree trunk fall inside to be thrown and flung about—never to escape.) But the wild animals and the people in the log could not harm the maiden, for she actually had not yet died.

The two continued along their way until they came to a great wall against which leaned a big cudgel. The young man took up the cudgel and hit the wall until it gave way, yielding them passage. This wall is called *taiyáya*. It borders the Land of the Dead. Only those dead whom Kopecho has sent along the path of the righteous can break through this wall. The girl kept all these things in mind and followed her lover until finally they came to a very wide river. They did not need to wait long before they saw a huge dog on the opposite shore. The beast promptly jumped into the water and swam across to them. He bade the girl swim over without fear, while he told the young man to hold fast to one of his ears to be towed. Without the help of the dog no dead person can reach the other shore, for he would be swallowed by the waters and drowned. Often the dead are forced to wait a long time before the dog comes to tow them across. These are they who have mistreated dogs during their lifetime on earth, and this is why the Yupa do not beat their dogs.

Having safely reached the other side of the river, they both continued on their way. By now, however, they were no longer in the land between the living and the dead, but had finally entered the Land of the Dead itself. Soon they saw the first village of many round huts. Here a multitude of dead, all of which had the appearance of human beings, gathered around the couple. In the meantime, the young man himself had assumed human form once again. They all asked the girl how it was that she had reached the Land of the Dead without first having died. The young man related how on his journey he had been called back by the sorrowful lamentation of the girl even before he had reached the wide river; and how she had then followed him without fear. Then he told them how the Lord of the Frogs had let them find each other again, even though he was offended by the girl's poorly made basket. Those dwelling in the Land of the Dead were highly pleased and arranged a great feast. They asked the girl when she planned to return. She answered that she enjoyed living with them and that she would like to stay for several years.

Toward the end of this period the dead arranged another great feast to mark the departure of their guest. She had come to feel that she had actually been staying with live people, for the dead conducted themselves exactly as did the living. They ate just like them and also had plenty to eat. They lived in family groups, had sexual relations with one another and had children. But not one of those who dwelt in the Land of the Dead attempted to have intercourse with the girl, because under the circumstances she would have died.

After the farewell celebration the girl set out on her way home. She went alone and came once more to the spot where years before her lover had been shot and buried. Here she found members of her own tribe full of curiosity. They questioned her, but she betrayed nothing to them of what had befallen her in the Land of the Dead.

Full of joy over the return of their daughter, the parents arranged a great feast, for which an abundance of food and drink was prepared. Like the others, the girl enjoyed the strong drink offered. Soon she became so intoxicated that she lost control of her thoughts, and thus revealed all that she had seen and experienced in the Land of the Dead. Later, when she returned to her senses, they told her what she had done. Thinking that now her lover would reject her, she was so overcome with sadness that in her grief she seized an arrow and, thrusting it into her body, she killed herself.

Summary: *The Land of the Dead*

A girl mourns her dead lover. He returns to take her to the Land of the Dead. Kopecho sends them each along a different path to test the girl's worthiness. She is attacked by animals and people but finally rejoins her lover. After several years in the Land of the Dead the girl returns home. On drinking too much at a feast, she reveals everything she has seen. Realizing her misdeed, she kills herself in grief.

Motif Content:	*The Land of the Dead*
B151.	Animal determines road to be taken.
C112.	Tabu: sexual intercourse with unearthly beings.
C423.3.	Tabu: revealing experiences in otherworld.
E310.	Dead lover's friendly return.

E420.+.	Revenant as cloud and wind. (E420. Appearance of revenant.)
E481.2.	Land of the dead across water.
E545.13.	Man converses with dead.
E752.5.+.	Dogs accompany soul to otherworld (E752.5. Hell-hounds accompany soul to lower world.)
F101.	Return from lower world.
F141.1.	River as barrier to otherworld.
F148.	Wall around otherworld.
F150.3.	Challenge at entrance of otherworld.
F151.1.	Perilous path to otherworld.
F151.1.3.	Perilous forest on way to otherworld.
F151.1.4.	Perilous fork on way to otherworld.
F152.	Bridge to otherworld.
F163.	Buildings in otherworld.
F168.	Villages in otherworld.
H1250.1.	Test of hero before journey to otherworld.
H1569.	Tests of character—misc.
N741.	Unexpected meeting of husband and wife.
W181.	Jealousy.

7. THE ORIGIN OF TUBERS AND BANANAS*

Once upon a time a father went hunting with his three sons. High up in the mountains they spied a wild boar which ran past them while actually quite some distance away. The father should have shot it, but since he missed his target he ordered his sons to wait there until he returned from his search for the lost arrow. He left and searched at length, but in vain, so that finally he gave up the search and sought to return to his sons. Only then did he notice that his wanderings had led him astray in a mountain range criss-crossed with canyons and chasms. Despite his great effort to find the right path again he failed completely. Meanwhile the sons sought their father in vain, assuming finally that he had tumbled over one of the cliffs. They returned home much grieved to report the sad incident to the village.

Now the father went his errant way through the forest for many

*See also narrative 42 and note to narrative 2.

days and many nights. One day, right in the middle of the forest, he found a hammock slung between two trees. Overjoyed to have found human beings once more, he sat down near the hammock and waited for its owner. At last he heard footsteps. A young man was coming toward him. The owner of the hammock was greatly astonished at the presence of the man and asked him how it was that he had found his way to that particular spot. The man related what had happened on the hunt, and then asked for the way to his village. At this the young man laughed, revealing to him that he was no longer on earth at all; that quite the contrary he was now in heaven. Then he introduced himself as the son of the moon, and invited the man to come with him to the house of his father.

On their way to the moon, the two were discovered by the sun, who straightway sought to take possession of the human, wishing to devour him. But the son of Moon stood protectively in front of the Yupa and shielded him from the sun's clutches, arguing that Sun had no right at all to the human since he himself had discovered the Yupa first.

At this the sun retreated so that the two wanderers were able to continue their way, arriving finally at the house of Moon after a long journey. Here the Yupa was introduced by his protector to Moon, who received the stranger as his guest with exceedingly great joy.

The Yupa lived in the house of the moon for four years, at the end of which time he begged his host to allow him to return to his own people on earth. The moon granted this wish. He gave the man shoots of yuca, yams, plantain, and cotton seeds as gifts for him to plant following his return to earth. Then Moon showed him the right path, and the Yupa set out on his way home.

Now it happened that the sons of this man were hunting again in the same place, just as they had done so many years before. Suddenly they saw their heavily laden father coming toward them. They could hardly believe their eyes. Overjoyed, they accompanied him to the village, there to do as he commanded them. They planted all the shoots which he had brought. From that time on the Yupa had fields of yuca, yams, and cooking bananas. And from that time on cotton also grew upon this earth. It is from this cotton that the Yupa make their clothes.

Summary: *The Origin of Tubers and Bananas*
Once a hunter gets lost in the forest. There he meets the son of the moon who brings him to the moon. After four years he returns home, bringing cotton seeds and shoots of yuca, yams, and bananas.

Motif Content:	*The Origin of Tubers and Bananas*
A711.2.	Sun as a cannibal.
A1423.4.	Acquisition of manioc.
A2684.3.	Origin of cotton plant.
A2686.4.3.	Origin of yams.
A2687.5.	Origin of banana.
F16.	Visit to land of moon.
N350.+.	Accidental loss of arrow. (N350. Accidental loss of property.)
N771.+.	Man lost on hunt has adventures. (N771. King [prince] lost on hunt has adventures.)

8. IN THE LAND OF THE DWARFS

When a Yupa dies, all his friends and kin come together to talk about him, to reminisce, to weep and wail. And so it was once upon a time when a man died: they came one and all, prepared the body, and carried it to the ossary of the tribe. The cave was large enough for all mourners to enter, to lay the bones down among those of his forefathers.

Just as everybody had stepped into the cave, the mountain suddenly trembled. Great stones blocked the opening to the cave. Big boulders fell upon the people, killing and crushing them. Only a few lived through the earthquake. Once again all was still. The survivors sought escape but the stones were too heavy to be moved. Forced to accept their lot, the trapped Yupa died, one after another.

Finally, only one man remained alive. He did not give up hope. Still looking for some way out he had climbed over the bones of his ancestors, far into the interior of the cave. Here he found, as he had hoped, a narrow crack between two great rocks leaning against each other. He was just able to slip between these to freedom.

Total darkness reigned outside. It was night. So the Indian sat down to wait for dawn to find his way back to the village in the morning. What a sad story he would have to tell those who had stayed behind!

At the crack of dawn the man sought to find his way home. But to his great surprise he realized that he was not in his native land at all. He had entered a strange world. All day long he searched for some familiar path. In vain! Trees, rivers, animals, all were the same as those at home, and yet everything was strange to him. In the afternoon he succeeded in shooting a bird which he roasted and ate toward evening.

As his fire burned lower, he settled down to sleep in the shelter of a rock. Suddenly, from the other side of the rock, he heard the sound of human voices.

He climbed on top of the rock to find out if the voices were those of Yupa or of enemies. Looking down over the edge of the rock he saw a circular area beneath, ringed with blocks of stone. A great fire billowed in the center, and in its glow rose a thick column of smoke around which many small people danced. With arms raised, and bending forward from the waist, they inhaled great gulps of the heavy smoke from the fire. And so the Yupa knew that, on passing through the cave of the dead, he had entered by chance into the land of the Pïpïntu. It could be nothing else. Here were the dwarfs dancing before his very eyes, nourishing themselves from the smoke of the fire, and sporting long beards, but without hair on their heads (which they lost because the waste of all humanity falls down upon their heads from the world above).

The Yupa had nothing to fear from these dwarfs, so he climbed down from the rock and drew near the dancing Pïpïntu. Somewhat afraid, they backed off on seeing the tall human, but gave him a friendly welcome nevertheless.

The Yupa told his hosts all that had happened to him: how he was the only one to come out of the cave of the dead, and how he had searched in vain the whole day long to find his way back to his people in the upper world. The dwarfs invited him to stay a while and gather new strength. After that they would show him the way back to his land.

The Yupa spent a long time in the Underworld of the dwarfs, who hardly differed from humans in their manner of living except in the fact that they obtained the greater part of their nourishment from the smoke of their fire. They took solid food in a strange and unusual fashion. That is to say, in eating meat or some other fare, the dwarfs squatted down, laid the food on the back of their necks, and let it slide down their backbones. They drank water the usual way. The Yupa was very surprised when one day he discovered that the dwarfs had no anus. For their part, the dwarfs were astonished to discover this feature in their guest. The more they watched the Yupa put food into his mouth, the more they envied him his physical constitution.

Why could they not also experience the full joy of food after all the trouble and work it took to get it? Why, indeed, should they have to let food simply roll down their backs instead of eating it?

One day the Pïpïntu chief came to his guest with a great request. Could not the dwarfs also acquire an anus by means of some sort of operation? He bade the Yupa to try this on one of the boys of the tribe. At first the Yupa refused, for he feared such an undertaking might kill the boy. But the dwarfs stood firm behind their leader; they begged and pestered the Indian until he finally gave in. They even promised that they would not hold it against him should he fail in his task. So the Yupa took an arrow tip of bone in his hand and carved the Pïpïntu lad a fold in his seat and a little hole in the proper place.

The boy experienced a good deal of pain, but otherwise he seemed to suffer no ill effects from the operation. On the following day, however, the boy died after he had consumed food by mouth.

In spite of this, the Pïpïntu clung to their desire. They brought another boy to the Yupa—he died. Another—he died. Still another—he died. Many died. All died. However, none died immediately after the operation. They died on the following day, after food had been taken by mouth instead of rolling it down the back. They had not died because of the new anus in their behinds. They died because they lacked the intestines, and because of the food pressing from inside their bodies.

After this sad experience, the Pïpïntu realized that, as dwarfs of the Underworld, they were destined to eat differently from the Yupa in the world above. True to their promise, they continued to treat their guest with great friendliness. They even offered him one of their most beautiful maidens as a wife, and in her company the Indian tarried many days longer with the Pïpïntu.

But the Yupa could not feel at home with the dwarfs. Being built as he was, he was always aware of how different their bodies were: this strange way they had of eating, and the daily dance around the smoking fire! Finally he begged them to show him the way to the world of his people. According to the promise, they agreed and after a long journey they came to a place where two paths crossed. Here the Yupa and his wife bade farewell to the friendly Pïpïntu and climbed through a crack in the rocks back into the world of human beings. How happy he was to find himself once more in his old, familiar land. In a short time he was again among his own people.

His Pïpïntu wife bore him a great number of children. To be sure, these did not grow to be as large as the Yupa children, but otherwise they were made exactly the same. From these very children are descended all the small people who are to be found today in the Sierra de Perijá.

Summary: *In the Land of the Dwarfs*

A Yupa, trapped in a burial cave, finally escapes and comes to the land of the dwarfs. He spends years there and marries a dwarf woman. The dwarfs eat by rolling the food down their backbones, and they have no anus. They ask the Yupa to make them like him through an operation, but this fails. Finally the Yupa returns to his country.

Motif Content:	*In the Land of the Dwarfs*
F92.6.	Entrance to lower world through cave.
F167.2.	Dwarfs in otherworld.
F183.+.	Dwarfs eat smoke. (F183. Foods in otherworld.)
F451.1.	Origin of dwarfs.
F451.2.3.1.	Long-bearded dwarfs.
F451.2.4.+.	Dwarfs have no hair. (F451.2.4. The hair of dwarfs.)
F451.5.1.	Helpful dwarfs.
F451.5.23.	Dwarfs seek human help in their fights and troubles.
F451.6.3.4.	Dwarf dances.
F529.2.+.	Dwarfs have no anus. (F529.2. People without anuses.)

F561.	People of unusual diet.
J1919.	Fatal disregard of anatomy—misc.
T111.5.	Marriage of mortal and dwarf.

9. THE YUPA AND THE MANAPSA

Once upon a time a Yupa Indian fell in love with a maiden of the Manapsa tribe. He had already started a family among the Yupa, but he deserted his wife and his children, and followed the girl to the village of the Manapsa, where they lived together for a long time.

Once during a great feast (which the Manapsa celebrate with much food and with *kusháre),* the Yupa remembered the family he had forsaken for his new young wife. The thought made him sad. His sadness grew until finally he decided to return to his Yupa family. When he told his young Manapsa wife she said she agreed, at least so it seemed. She bade him stay but one day longer, however, so that he might sleep off the effects of the great party and strengthen himself with food.

The following day the Yupa took leave of his young wife and her kindred and set upon his way. He had not gone far when he felt a sudden rush of blood in his ears. Terrible headaches tortured him. Suddenly he realized that the Manapsa had poisoned him.

Now it happened that this Yupa Indian was a *tuano—*a medicine man—and his Yupa wife was a *tuana.* So as soon as he felt the poison within him he speedily sought a certain herb. (The sap of this weed works against the effects of the poison.) Fortunately he found the weed after a short time and chewed it up, and with his last bit of strength he dragged himself home.

His wife received him with great joy. Because she was a *tuana,* she saw right away that her husband was more dead then alive. Together they thought about which herbs were best suited to combat the poison in the body of the man. The *tuana* herself went to look for some. Soon she had found the plants and had brewed a potion from their juices. "Drink this," said the *tuana,* "and you shall not die." She also suggested that they leave the village and move far away from the Manapsa. Thereupon she wove a great basket, put her sick husband into it, and carried

90

him away over the hills. The man drank the potion along the way and felt better with each passing day. When they were finally a good distance removed from the land of the Manapsa, his recovery was complete. They came upon a house in the mountains and there they lived all alone.

As time went by the *tuano* recovered and became very silent. He thought and thought about how he could get even with the Manapsa.

One day he went into the forest and felled a tree. By hollowing out the trunk he made two little caskets, and fitted each with a cover. Next he set out to look for beehives. Finally he found two of the male *arigua* and two of the female *arigua*. He and his wife ate up the honey. He melted the wax and mixed it with ashes. Then he went to the burying place, gathered up the bones of two children—those of a girl and those of a boy—and carried them home. He set the bones in position and poured the liquid wax over them. He placed each of the wax children in a box and closed each with the corresponding lid.

The following day he ordered his wife, the *tuana,* to pick up the box with the girl inside, while he himself picked up the one with the boy. The *tuana* had long known what her husband planned. She did what he asked without question.

For a long time the two kept going until one day, toward evening, they approached the Manapsa village. They set the wax children in their boxes under a tree, covered them with palm leaves, and then went again into the forest unseen by their enemies.

In the middle of the night, however, the boxes opened. A myriad of *karau* (evil spirits of the night) burst from them and streaked off howling towards the Manapsa village. All those Manapsa who heard their shrieking perished on the spot. Only a few escaped. Thus did the Yupa take revenge on the Manapsa. The tribe was wiped out.

The *karau* then attacked the villages of the Yupa. All the Indians ran to their mighty *tuano,* begging him for protection. The *tuano* built a huge house right away. All the Yupa gathered together inside, for the thick walls of leaves kept out the shrieking and howling of the *karau.* Next, he and his wife went into the woods to look for certain herbs. They sprinkled the sap of these plants over the several pathways leading into the village. The *karau* shrank back, and ever since have had a great fear of the Yupa. They fled. The Yupa were thus later able to settle on the land where their old neighbors, the Manapsa, had formerly lived.

Summary: *The Yupa and the Manapsa*

A Yupa has deserted his family to live with a Manapsa woman in his tribe. When he decides to return his new wife poisons him, but he is cured by his Yupa wife. To get even with the Manapsa he lets loose, through witchcraft, a horde of evil spirits on their village and wipes out the tribe. When the spirits then attack his own tribe he scares them away.

Motif Content:	*The Yupa and the Manapsa*
D1381.	Magic object protects from attack.
D1402.19.	Magic statue kills.
D2061.	Magic murder.
K951.0.1. +.	Deserted wife poisons departing husband. (K951.0.1. Deserted wife chokes departing husband.)
K2231.	Treacherous mistress.
Q211.8.	Punishment for desire to commit murder.
S111.+.	Attempted murder by poisoning. (S111. Murder by poisoning.)

10. THE ORIGIN OF THE WHITES AND THEIR TECHNOLOGY

One day a Yupa woman found a stone from which she made a phallus. By having relations with this stone she finally got herself with child and bore a daughter. The other members of her tribe found it most amazing that a woman alone could bear a child and resolved in the future to keep watch over her wanderings. And thus they discovered the secret of her conception and birth.

One day when the woman went into the forest to seek fruits, they took away the stone and shattered it on a rock. To their great surprise, blood came forth from the broken pieces. When the woman returned from her food quest and found what the men had done, she became very sad. She mourned the broken stone as if it had been her husband who had died, refused all food and drink, and finally perished.

Her daughter, although she was still quite small, understood everything that had happened. Day after day she scolded the people for the death of her parents. Finally she became so embittered that she was determined to destroy all the Yupa. At the age of three she began to make the oddest things, things which even the adult Yupa had never seen in their lives, and which they really had no idea how to make. She used a hard material for which the Yupa did not even know the name—something that the whites call "iron". She made machines and shooting weapons in great numbers. All this was for one purpose only: to eventually kill all the Yupa.

Not only the Yupa, but also God looked with anxious eyes on the doings of the girl. On the one hand he did not want to let her carry out her plan, but on the other hand he was far from pleased with what he knew to be the plan of the Yupa, who, fearing the girl because of her arts, had decided to kill her.

So God sent one of his servants, the king vulture, to earth to take the girl away from the Yupa people. When he came down to earth, the vulture changed himself into a man and mingled with the Yupa. Before many days had passed he had won the trust of the adults and could secretly tell them that he had come to save them from the danger of the girl, and that, furthermore, he desired to take her away with him. The Yupa could only agree with him, just so long as they might be free of the child.

Next the king vulture approached the girl, indicating the attachment he felt for her. One day he told her that he had to go on his way and asked her if she would like to come along. The girl, not caring much for the company of the Yupa, agreed right away and joined him gladly; but she made sure that she would be allowed to return once in a while to visit the village. He packed into a great basket everything she had produced thus far and whatever else she possessed. Indeed he was careful to make certain that none of her goods and chattle were left behind. The Yupa let them go without bidding them farewell.

Along the way the vulture stopped at a great tree and made a ladder of netted cotton. "We want to go up here," he said. "The way across the mountains is too irksome." Then he threw the ladder over the tree and asked the girl to climb up ahead with the basket. Finally she stood high up in the top of the tree. Then the king vulture pulled upon the ladder so that it fell down, thus cutting off her way back to earth. On seeing herself so deceived by mankind and by the king vulture, the girl wept and wept many long days and nights until a great sea was formed by her tears. The water covered great portions of the earth and would certainly also have flooded our land had not the lagoon (Lake Maracaibo) caught the water on its shores.

Finally the girl ceased weeping, took her basket, and made off, stepping out over the water. It was a long, long way across the sea. During the journey the girl became a young woman. She conceived a child by the water.

Finally she reached the farther shore and there gave birth to an infant whose father was the sea, and whose skin was as white as the water. This child grew to manhood and from him issued other children, all born of his own mother. Thus came into being all those many people whose skin is white in color. Like their ancestral mother, they also began to make all sorts of complicated things from iron, like machines and firearms. The Yupa understand nothing of these things, because they no longer had anybody who could teach them. However, this was their just punishment for having broken the stone to pieces.

Summary: *The Origin of the Whites and Their Technology*

A girl wants to destroy all Yupa for killing her mother and a stone phallus considered her father. For this purpose she makes many firearms, using iron. To save her the Yupa God sends the king vulture, who lures her up into a tree and then abandons her. Finally the girl conceives a son, with very white skin, by the sea formed from her tears. Thus originated the whites. They know about machines but the Yupa do not; this is their punishment.

Motif Content:	*The Origin of the Whites and Their Technology*
A1459.1.+.	Origin of white man's weapons. (A1459.1. Acquisition of weapons.)
A1614.9.	Origin of white man.
B455.1.	Helpful vulture.
D2125.1.	Magic power to walk on water.
F809.4.	Bleeding rock.
K710.	Victim enticed into voluntary captivity or helplessness.

K1113.+.	Abandonment on tree. (K1113. Abandonment on stretching tree.)
N810.4.	Supernatural helper comes from sky.
R111.6.	Girl rescued and then abandoned.
T211.9.	Excessive grief at husband's or wife's death.
T523.+.	Conception from water. (T523. Conception from bathing.)
T539.6.*	Conception from artificial phallus.

11. THE IRAPA AND THE PARIRÍ

For a long time the Irapa and the Parirí were enemies because a Parirí man had killed five Irapa families.

This Parirí had two wives and six children. All of a sudden long hair began to grow over his entire body. He was mocked by his own people, and to escape their ridicule the man became a loner. He went out hunting all day long, returning home with his booty only after night had fallen. He would then eat and sleep, only to be gone again before the break of day.

One morning his wives noticed that one of their six children was missing. The following morning another child was gone; on the next morning still another, until all the children had vanished. Then both women disappeared as well; in this way an entire family was eliminated.

Naturally the people of the village suspected the sinister lone hunter; yet they never discovered that he had not only killed his children and wives at midnight, but had also roasted and eaten them before the first light of dawn. However, they evacuated the camp and no longer bothered with their hairy tribesman.

Several days after the Parirí had left their camp a group of five Irapa families drew near it. With loud shouts they made known their approach from afar. The sole Parirí, who had stayed behind, answered and invited them to come into the village. He entertained them and told them that his people had gone to a neighboring village to participate in a festival. They should pass the night with him, and then follow the others along to the next village on the following day.

But while the Irapa lay sleeping, the Parirí took a great club

*Assignment of new motif number.

95

and with it slew his guests one after the other. When day dawned the dreadful deed was done. To keep the flesh from spoiling too quickly, he dragged the bodies into the shade of the forest nearby.

Next morning the brother of the murderer came to the camp and found the Irapa lying dead in the woods. He woke his brother, who had fallen asleep after his strenuous labor, and asked him the whereabouts of the guests who had announced their arrival the evening before. "They were only passing through," was the reply. Thus the man found out that his brother was the murderer of the Irapa. He took his leave and went home. But after that he warned all Irapa, who announced their intention to visit the homestead of his brother from far away, not to go near the village.

Several months later a number of Irapa warriors came to the murderer's brother and revealed to him that they had come to avenge the death of their people. The Pariri knew well that the Irapa were justified. He would, therefore, not attempt to protect his brother; yet, on the other hand, he could not in clear conscience help them accomplish this deed. He bade them, furthermore, to kill his brother in their own territory, rather than in the land of the Pariri. The Irapa promised this and went off to the murderer's camp where their tribesmen had been massacred.

From quite some distance away they announced their coming with loud shouting, and the murderer invited them to come into the village. They had scarcely arrived, though, when they surprised the murderer, took him captive, and bound his arms together.

The following day they set off on their way home taking the prisoner along. They passed by a cave where two heavy clubs lay hidden. The murderer begged the Irapa to give him the chance to destroy these clubs. But the Irapa immediately recognized the evil intention of the Pariri and pushed him along. That night, as he lay sleeping, they killed him with their arrows.

Summary: *The Irapa and the Pariri*

An outcast Pariri man kills his family, one by one. One night he also kills, through treachery, five Irapa families. His brother finds this out and allows Irapa warriors to capture and kill the murderer in revenge.

Motif Content:	*The Irapa and the Pariri*
F521.1.	Man covered with hair like animal.

G77.+.	Husband eats wife and children. (G77. Husband eats wife.)
K834.+.	Victims killed while asleep in killer's camp. (K834. Victim killed while asleep in killer's house.)
K2294.	Treacherous host.
Q411.6.	Death as punishment for murder.

12. PARERACHA—THE RED STONE

One day a woman found a great, reddish slab of stone on the bank of the river. It shone most wonderfully. How happy she would be if she could rub the very same color on her own body.

So she searched and found a rough stone which she used to scrub the stone slab, back and forth, until there was a little pile of red powder. She mixed some water with the powder. Then she colored her body with the shining red. Standing there so beautifully painted she began to sing for very joy. And as she sang, the stone slab on which she stood opened and swallowed her up.

Even today, on passing this stone, one can still hear the song of the enchanted woman.

Summary: *Pareracha—The Red Stone*
Woman who paints herself with powder from a red stone is swallowed by the stone.

Motif Content:	*Pareracha—the Red Stone*
F807.1.+.	Red rock. (F807.1. Crimson rock.)
F943.1.+.	Woman sinks into stone. (F943.1. Man sinks into stone.)

13. ATAPOINSHA, THE INVISIBLE WAR HERO

One day when the Yupa sought to move into a new land, they found it occupied by the powerful tribe of the Meteru. They probably would have had to fight for some time against this enemy, had not Atapoinsha lived among them. He was a Yupa who could make himself invisible.

So they sent this man out against the Meteru. Atapoinsha walked to within a few steps of the enemy and then shot off his arrows, as fast as lightning. He did this every day until the Meteru, seized by panic, fled down the Yasa river to the valley. But in their blind retreat they did not notice that, down where the Negro flows into the Santa Ana, there is a swamp and the Lagoon of the Dead Waters. They fell into the morass and all of them perished.

Now the Yupa, following in quick pursuit, also came near the lagoon. As they ran shouting after those who fled, they suddenly noticed how the waters echoed their cries, and in this way they were warned of the danger. Halting in midstride, they found their enemy destroyed. Since this time the Yupa have lived in the mountains of Perijá, and the Barí, the few descendants of the Meteru, live in the part further to the south of the Sierra.

Summary: *Atapoinsha, the Invisible War Hero*
The Yupa acquire their present territory by the help of an invisible man who chases the former occupants into the swamps.

Motif Content:	*Atapoinsha, the Invisible War Hero*
A526.7	Culture hero performs remarkable feats of strength and skill.
A1620.	Distribution of tribes.
D1980.	Magic invisibility.
Q467.3. + .	Drowning in swamp. (Q467.3. Punishment: drowning in swamp.)

14. AN ATTACK OF THE METERU

One day the men left the settlement to go on a hunting drive together. When toward evening they had still not returned, the wives became concerned and took precautions to protect themselves from an eventual attack by the Meteru. They ran into the woods and brought great quantities of dried leaves together which they piled up all around the camp.

In the night a group of Meteru warriors drew near. They wanted to attack the encampment of their enemy in order to abduct the women. Without paying attention to what they were doing they stepped into the heaps of dry leaves, and an old Yupa woman woke up from her light sleep and softly alarmed all her sleeping companions. These took their children and fled into the forest, after a young woman with bow and arrow had taken her position behind a thick tree. She killed the first Meteru who stepped into the village, and then fled unseen into the forest while the enemy gathered around the fallen warrior.

Next morning when the women returned to the village, they found that the corpse of the Meteru was no longer there; only a pool of blood remained in the spot where he had fallen. On the strength of that the women fled with their children into a neighboring village.

Toward midday the Yupa returned home from the hunt. Shortly before they reached the village they came across an Indian in the woods, who had participated in the attack and had then lost his way. He did not present himself as a Meteru, but rather as the member of another tribe, and begged the Yupa for some fire so that he might prepare himself an anteater. The Yupa helped him and then continued on their way. Thus the Meteru escaped.

Summary: *An Attack of the Meteru*

Yupa women, alone in their village, are attacked by the Meteru. They kill one enemy and then flee. Returning Yupa men unwittingly help a Meteru to escape.

Motif Content:	*An Attack of the Meteru*
F565.	Women warriors or hunters.
J670.	Forethought in defenses against others.
K500.	Escape from death or danger by deception.
K778.1.	Amazon overcomes enemies singly.

15. THE GREAT DYING

In earlier times there were many more Yupa Indians than there are today. They were all very healthy people and never suffered hunger.

One day an evil spirit, Botono, appeared in their land. He flew over the tribal area of the Yupa with a choppy, harsh laugh and a dripping nose. Wherever the runny nose dripped, the people became sick throughout the village, for Botono is the spirit of the common cold.

First a woman died. They buried her and abandoned the village. After a short time, however, the Yupa heard someone roaming nightly through the new settlement and a voice calling: "Where have you gone?" Then they realized that this was the voice of the woman they had recently buried, and they ran to the abandoned village to see if perhaps she had come to life.

On entering the old village the following day, they were much surprised to see coming toward them the very woman they believed to be dead. When she stood close in front of them, she opened her mouth as if to speak to them. But before she had uttered one word she fell over dead! And so despite their puzzlement, there remained but little else for the men to do except bury her again.

However, this did not put an end to the strange happenings. The next night they heard the woman again as she wandered through their village, loudly calling the names of her family: "Where have you gone?" The Yupa were seized by a terrible fear and this time no one wanted to return to the deserted village to investigate. Members of the family, however, did not agree with the general consensus of opinion, and did not wish to let the cry of their dead one go unanswered. So they went to the village, and, to be sure, they witnessed the very same events that had happened the day before.

Toward evening, after they had returned to the new village, all the Yupa concluded that although the woman was indeed dead, her soul wished yet to remain among the living. Surely in time it would become resigned to its lot and give up the search.

During the night the woman came again and this time she complained even more than before. "Where have you gone?" she called over and over. She kept this up until the whole village agreed that they would go back and check once more on the following day, for the last time.

At the first grey light of morning all set out on their way: men, women, even the children. On arriving at the village they saw their relative coming toward them. Again it seemed as though she would speak to them, but she had scarcely opened her mouth when she fell over once again, and was dead. The Yupa recognized an ill omen. They buried the dead again and determined once and for all never to return to the old settlement. Furthermore, they decided that they would move far away, to a place where the dead one could not follow them.

On the way to the new tribal grounds the great dying of the Yupa began. First the children died, then the women, then the men. All of them died, for the *tuano* had no remedy to fight this sickness.

In this great dying only two *tuanos* were spared, one man and one woman. Although wasted to the very bone, they never ceased to hope . . . The question of how to rid the world of Botono's evil continuously puzzled their minds. They determined to look for a very special kind of plant, which up to then had not been tried. They squeezed this and let the juice trickle into the rivers so that it would be carried through the whole land. They also heated stones and threw them into the waters.

This "medicine" was finally successful. The two *tuanos* survived and from these two are descended all the Yupa of today. They had many children and these were allowed to marry amongst each other until the Yupa tribe became numerous once again. Then came the day when the *tuano* wished to re-establish the old order: in the future the Yupa were forbidden to marry within the small family circle. In spite of the strong stand he took regarding the old order, many Yupa did not wish to live by these rules.

One day the sun grew dark and rain began to pour down in torrents. The Yupa knew immediately that the cause of the bad weather was to be laid squarely on the shoulders of the many men and women who had disobeyed the *tuano*. The actual sinners did not dare to leave their houses during the many, many days it rained without stopping. All were very hungry. So they begged those, who had not sinned against the incest tabu, to go out to the fields to gather food. These people put great *plantanilla* leaves on their heads, and, taking resinous torches in hand, tried to reach their fields. But because the great masses of water flooded the valleys with such force, the soil together with all the crops of the field had been swept away. Thus the Yupa searching for food found nothing but bare rocks where there were formerly plants. A great famine arose, and many Yupa died from hunger and from cold.

The survivors looked with great anxiety to their *tuano*, hoping that he might summon the strength to set aright this wretched state of affairs. The *tuano* sank into deep contemplation. On the first day the black clouds withdrew and behind a blanket of grey clouds the sun could be seen at its zenith. Its normal course through the heavens had been interrupted. The sun stood still.

The *tuano* concentrated intensely, praying and pleading ceaselessly. Suddenly he rose from the earth to make the long journey
to the sun. He climbed higher and higher, and each day it rained
less.

Finally the *tuano* reached the sun. He laid himself against the
sun's head, begging, beseeching. All the while the sun grew more
and more bright and it rained less and less on earth. Finally the
sun resumed its usual size and at this point took up its normal
path once more. The Yupa cheered as the *tuano* climbed down.
Nevertheless, he warned them not to live incestuously in the future.
"I do not know if I could ever again manage to drive away the
clouds and bring back the sun!"

Summary: *The Great Dying*

A woman killed by the evil spirit of the common cold comes
back to life three times. The frightened Yupa decide to move
far away. On the way, the cold kills all Yupa except two, whose
offspring multiply and form a new Yupa tribe. For breaking the
re-established incest tabu the Yupa are punished by a great rain
which causes famine. The medicine man saves them by calling
back the sun.

Motif Content:	*The Great Dying*
A1006.1.+.	New race from single pair (or several) after tribal calamity. (A1006.1. New race from single pair [or several] after world calamity.)
A1010.1.	Sun does not shine during deluge.
A1018.1.	Flood as punishment for breaking tabu.
A1018.2.	Flood as punishment for incest.
A1028.	Bringing deluge to end.
A1337.	Origin of disease.
A1337.0.2.+.	Disease caused by evil spirit. (A1337.0.2. Disease caused by ghosts.)
C114.	Tabu: incest.
D2161.1.+.	Magic control of specific diseases. (D2161.1. Magic cure for specific diseases.)
D2162.	Magic control of disease.
E151.	Repeated resuscitation.
F961.1.+.	Sun stands still. (F961.1. Extraordinary behavior of sun.)

K194. +.	Bargain: if the sun resumes its course. (K194.
	Bargain: if the sun reverses its course.)
Q552.3.1.	Famine as punishment.

16. THE CHICHA OF THE DWARFS

In early times the Yupa did not know how to brew well that *chicha* which makes people quite drunk. For this purpose they had the dwarfs, who even today make the best *chicha,* although they seldom get drunk.

Some time ago in a certain Yupa village there lived a dwarf, who was much teased and mocked because of his looks. One day the men ordered him to brew a great trough of the good *chicha.* In order to make his task more difficult they placed the trough so high up that he had to make himself a little ladder in order to reach it.

When the *chicha* was ready they took the ladder away from him. Thus he could not drink from the trough, but would have to content himself with what dripped down the sides. The dwarf declined, however, saying that actually he had no desire to drink. He took his gear and went fishing. Actually, he would have liked to drink *chicha* but he was proud, as are all the dwarfs. He was also afraid of the Yupa, who, during these bouts of drinking, are quick to strike and even to kill other people.

Summary: *The Chicha of the Dwarfs*

Since only dwarfs can make *chicha* villagers order a dwarf to brew them some. They then refuse to let him drink any of it.

Motif Content:	*The Chicha of the Dwarfs*
F451.5.1.7.	Dwarfs serve mortals.
F451.5.1.20.	Dwarfs help in performing task.
F451.5.11.	Dwarfs suffer abuses by mortals.
K2247.	Treacherous lord.

17. THE MAN WHO MARRIED HIS COUSIN*

One day a Manapsa came into the village of the Yupa and asked the people there to give him a wife. But right at that time there were no marriageable girls available, except for one—but she was a cousin (a parallel cousin) of the man who came courting. How-

*Possibly also his brother's daughter, i.e. his "niece".

ever, since the Yupa feared the anger of the Manapsa, they gave him the woman as his wife.

The young woman struggled with all her strength against this decision, but to no avail. Several days later she had to pack her things and follow the man into the village of the Manapsa.

On the way the man unsuccessfully tried to win the affections of the woman and to have intercourse with her. She would not submit, however, and scolded him soundly. With this he lost patience, and suddenly pretended to have gotten something in his eye. As the woman stepped near to help him remove the object he grabbed her, threw her to the ground, and urinated in her vagina. The humiliated woman ran home, told her people what had happened, and died soon thereafter.

Now the *tuanos* of both these groups had to prepare their people for the anticipated battle. They bathed men, women, and children in a plant juice especially prepared for that purpose. Soon the Yupa invited the Manapsa to come into their village to take part in a festivity. The Manapsa accepted the invitation, although they knew that it would end in a fight. Soon after their arrival the struggle began. The men shot each other with arrows and the women beat each other with sticks. With the exception of a few men and women, who had not washed themselves carefully enough with the plant juices, no further casualties occurred—thanks to the protective measures taken by the *tuanos* of both sides.

Summary: *The Man Who Married His Cousin*

A Manapsa man forces his (parallel) cousin, a Yupa, into marriage and kills her when she resists him. In the resulting tribal war the medicine men's magic prevents large numbers of casualties.

Motif Content:	*The Man Who Married His Cousin*
C114.	Tabu: incest.
D1344.+.	Magic juice gives invulnerability. (D1344. Magic object gives invulnerability.)
K1326.	Seduction by feigned illness.
S62.	Cruel husband.
S139.+.	Husband kills wife by urinating in her vagina. (S139. Misc. cruel murders.)
T288.	Wife refuses to sleep with detested husband.
T410.+.	Incest between parallel cousins. (410. Incest.)

18. SLANDER

A man had two sisters who came to him daily in the field to cook for him there. The man, however, stayed evenings in the field, so that people started to whisper and ask each other how indeed he could spend the whole time with his sisters and leave his wife alone in the village with the children. Of course these rumors also spread to his spouse, and, although constantly defending her husband, the wife allowed on various occasions that at times she suspected something.

One day, as the two sisters were going home from the field, a man suddenly arose out of the ground before them and told them that the people in the village suspected them of carrying on with their brother in immodest ways, and that their sister-in-law had already accused them of this at different times.

Then the spectre sank again into the ground before the very eyes of the startled sisters, who continued on their way home. When they arrived they found their sister-in-law sleeping in the house, so they sat down in the shade of a Cacaruiti tree *(kurúishwu)* to think. Suddenly the ground beneath them opened and the girls disappeared into the abyss.

Many days had passed before the man finally came from the field to the village in order to find out what had happened to his sisters. But neither his wife nor any of the other people had seen them, and so the man set out immediately to seek some trace of the missing women.

On the way to the field he suddenly heard beautiful singing, which seemed to come from beneath the ground. Immediately he recognized the voices of his sisters and realized why it was they no longer lived on earth. Sadly he went to the fields, where he broke and buried everything that had belonged to his sisters. Then he left his tribe.

Summary: *Slander*

Two women, accused of having relations with their brother, disappear into the ground.

Motif Content:	*Slander*
E546.	The dead sing.
K2100.	False accusation.
Q552.2.3.	Earth swallowings as punishment.
T415.	Brother-sister incest.

19. THE STINGY DAUGHTER-IN-LAW

One day a man went to visit his son and his daughter-in-law. The young man was very happy to see his father and told his wife to bring out the fresh snails she had gathered the day before.

But the woman wanted to keep all the snails for herself. She hid them and said there were none left. Nor did she offer her father-in law anything else, so that he soon became aware that he was an unwanted guest in that house. He said goodbye, promising to come back again at the birth of his first grandchild.

At the time of this visit, the young woman was already far gone with child, and a few days later her time came. Now during the birth there were many difficulties, one after the other. The mother lost the baby, together with her entire womb, and then she lost all her insides.

As she lay dying she called all her relatives and told her father-in-law where she had hidden the snails. Then all present knew why these things had happened—but who would still have wanted the snails!

They left the dead woman lying there without burial—so that at least the worms might get something from her.

Summary: *The Stingy Daughter-in-law*

A woman dies in childbirth for not having offered her father-in-law food when he visited her.

Motif Content:	*The Stingy Daughter-in-law*
Q276.	Stinginess punished.
Q411.	Death as punishment.
Q415.3. +.	Punishment: woman eaten by worms. (Q415.3. Punishment: man eaten by worms [snake].)
W152.	Stinginess.

20. BAD DREAMS

A long time ago among the Yupa lived a man, who distinguished himself because of his diligence. Every morning he went to the field even before sunrise, and returned only after sunset.

One night he dreamed that he was roving around among the houses in the village while continually playing a flute of the dead. Next morning he woke up somewhat later than usual and made his way to the field.

On the way, a big worm *(gusano cabezón, makaane)* fastened itself to his garment, and climbing up his leg attached itself firmly between the man's legs. To be sure the latter felt a slight pain, but he did not pay any further attention to it.

Within a few days, the worm grew to a gigantic size and sucked so much blood out of the man that he died. When his children drew his mantle from him, they were horrified to see the great worm, which they immediately removed and killed.

Although everybody had liked the diligent man very much indeed, many said that he had died through his own stupidity. They were right: for if one should dream of flutes of the dead, jumping snakes, red batata, red stones, or even of Karau, the bad night-spirit, then one just does not ever leave the house.

Summary: *Bad Dreams*
A man, who has dreamed of the flute of the dead, is killed by a worm sucking out his blood.

Motif Content:	*Bad Dreams*
D1810.8.3.1.	Warning in dream fulfilled.
D1810.8.3.2.	Dream warns of danger which will happen in near future.
D1812.3.3.5.	Prophetic dream allegorical.
D1812.5.1.2.	Bad dream as evil omen.
Q415.3.	Punishment: man eaten by worms (snake).

21. BLOOD FEUD

An old man fell ill. Since he no longer had a wife, he asked his sister to come and care for him for as long as the illness lasted. She agreed, although quite reluctantly, and only because everybody expected this service of her. The sickness dragged on for quite some time. The woman often grumbled, especially because she had both her sick brother and his son to care for.

One day she set out to make *pamocha*. She burned a quantity of stalks of the royal palm, sieved water through the ashes, and then boiled down the liquid. She put the salt that had remained on a roll of tobacco and gave it to her old brother to chew for a quid. The sick one was very happy over this special labor of love and chewed away the whole day. In the evening his condition grew worse, and then toward midnight he expired in great pain.

Now the woman believed that only she herself knew why her

brother had died so suddenly. But the nephew had witnessed exactly what had happened—how she had mixed a poisonous juice made of fish and leaves in with the *pamocha*. His sick father had noticed a difference, namely that the *pamocha* had turned out somewhat bitter, but he took it anyway because he wanted to keep his sister in a good humor.

During the festival of the dead which followed, much *chicha* was consumed, and all the men, women and children became drunk. As the feast reached its climax, one of the partakers suddenly fell over dead. An arrow shot by an unknown hand had struck him in the breast. The dead man was a nephew of the old man who had just passed away, a son of the sister who had cared for the ill man so long. Now the sister had still another brother with whom she got along well, and this man warned her that the murderer would come again and kill her, too; she really should move away to another village.

The woman was frightened; she packed her things together, and made her way to a neighboring village. On the way, however, a still greater fear of the unknown murderer settled upon her, so she turned around and went back to her own village.

"I do not think that he will kill me," she said to her brother. "I am a woman."

However, her nephew made preparations to kill her. Toward evening he went to the house of his aunt for supper, as he had on other days. She fixed *ocumo* and gave him some. At the first opportunity, however, the nephew spilled the vegetable on the floor and trod it underfoot. He feared the poison of his aunt.

After eating, everyone lay down to sleep, everyone that is, except the nephew. He put a peaked hat made of *caña brava* on his head, and tied his *manta* tight around his body. He would not sleep but sat up the whole night long.

When everyone had fallen asleep, he shot an arrow straight into his aunt's heart. She died instantly without so much as crying out. Then he quietly left the village and never came back again.

Summary: *Blood Feud*

A woman who has to care for her sick brother secretly poisons him. Her nephew takes revenge by killing her and her son.

Motif Content: *Blood Feud*
K2212.0.1.+.   Treacherous sister poisons brother.

	(K2212.0.0. Treacherous sister attempts to poison brother.)
Q211.9.	Fratricide punished.
Q411.6.	Death as punishment for murder.
S73.1.	Fratricide.
S74.1.+.	Nephew kills aunts. (S74.1. Nephew [niece] kills uncle.)
S111.	Murder by poisoning.

22. THE WOMAN WHO FISHED

One day a woman accompanied her husband to the river, where they fished together. Now, while they busied themselves in the water, the woman suffered the onset of her monthly bleeding. She sat down, without ceasing to fish.

But in sitting down she had overlooked a fish bone lying there on which a few green flies were laying their eggs. Some of these eggs entered the vagina of the woman where they developed into great maggots.

After several days the woman suffered great pains. She washed herself with hot water to ease the pain. To be sure most of the maggots were killed in this way, but a few others got as far as her heart. She stank horribly as she lay dying slowly. The Yupa were happy when they finally could bury that woman.

Summary: *The Woman Who Fished*

A menstruating woman who goes fishing is killed by maggots which enter her vagina.

Motif Content:	*The Woman Who Fished*
B784.1.	How animal gets into person's stomach (or body) (various methods).
C140.+.	Tabu: fishing during menses. (C140. Tabu connected with menses.)
Q415.3.+.	Punishment: woman eaten by worms.'(Q415.3. Punishment: man eaten by worms [snake].)

23. KONOCHTARI, THE CENTIPEDE

A man set out on a long journey with his wife. Evenings the wife spread out the straw mat, and they lay down to sleep.

One night the wife turned over in her sleep and slept on, face down. On this night Konochtari, the centipede, came up to her and crawled into her vagina.

The following night, when the man wanted to have intercourse with his wife, he became impotent and scolded her for having a biting vagina.

For a whole month long Konochtari lived inside the woman, producing a great number of offspring. When the woman began to menstruate again, Konochtari and his children left the vagina to go and eat *atamara* leaves. Then they went back again inside the woman. When they repeated this the second day the woman noticed what was going on, but it was already too late to keep back the intruders. So on the third day she went to the river and squatted down. However, as soon as all the Konochtari left her body, she jumped into the water, ridding herself of them in this way. But even so, her husband left her and nobody else wanted her thereafter.

Summary: *Konochtari, the Centipede*
Centipede crawls into woman's vagina, biting her husband's penis during intercourse. She gets rid of centipede but is rejected by husband and all other men.

Motif Content: *Konochtari, the Centipede*
B784.1. How animal gets into person's stomach (or body) (various methods).
F547.1.1. *Vagina dentata.*

24. THE DECEIVING MOTHER-IN-LAW

A young man had married and lived together with his wife and her mother in the same house.

One day the mother-in-law fell sick and could not get up from the mat. The man immediately sent his wife into the forest to get some special herbs. Many other herbs, which they also needed to cure this rare sickness of the mother-in-law, grew so high up in the mountains that the man himself had to climb about all day long in order to obtain them.

The mother-in-law took the medicine which her son-in-law prepared, but it did not help. The sickness lasted a very long time. At the beginning of the rainy season the man climbed up on the roof to repair some damage right above the place where the sick woman lay. At this time the woman asked for lots of water, which meant that her daughter was required to make several trips a day to the river in order to be able to give her as much fresh water as possible.

One day, when the young woman had just left again for the river, the mother-in-law called the man into the house. She pulled him down and begged him to lie next to her. Horrified, the man jumped to his feet and, running to his wife, told her all that had happened. The young woman was extremely angry and scolded her mother: "Night and day we care for you—seeking herbs, hauling water—and you aren't sick at all!"

The mother defended herself; she had only wanted to speak with the man. However, neither the young man nor his wife believed her.

"I shall not make any more medicine for you," he said.

"I shall give you no more to eat or drink," she said.

"If you are really ill, then die. But if you are in health, then get up and look after yourself!"

The mother-in-law was greatly ashamed. However, she did not die.

Summary: *The Deceiving Mother-in-law*

A young couple are nursing the wife's sick mother. Once, the mother tries to have intercourse with her son-in-law after which they refuse to take care of her.

Motif Content:	*The Deceiving Mother-in-law*
K1326.+.	Attempted seduction by feigned illness. (K1326. Seduction by feigned illness.)
K2218.	Treacherous relatives-in-law.
T417.1.+.	Mother-in-law seeks to seduce son-in-law. (T417.1. Mother-in-law seduces son-in-law.)

25. WHEN THERE WERE BUT FEW WOMEN

There was a time once when there were but a few women among the Yupa.

A man, who had no wife, decided one day to go into the forest and cut down five banana trees. He laid them down in a row, one next to the other, and on each he tied a loin cloth. Then he asked them:

"Are you thirsty?"

And he answered the question himself: "Yes!"

Thereupon he gave them something to drink. He then took a knife, lifted the loin cloth and carved a vagina in each of the five banana stems.

"You are now my wives!" he said. And the five wives laughed.

"You are not to suffer hunger, for I shall prepare a large field. Now eat!" The wives ate and were content with their husband. Every day he had intercourse with his wives; and every day he peeled off the dry top layer from the stems so that they would always be beautiful and smooth.

As the stems finally became very thin, there grew a new sprout next to each one of them, and the man recognized these as his children. He cared for them very well, and when the wives died, he took five new ones.

Summary: *When There Were But Few Women*

Long ago when there are few women among the Yupa, a man makes himself five wives from five banana trees.

Motif Content:	*When There Were But Few Women*
D431.2.	Transformation: tree to person.
D435.1.1.	Transformation: statue comes to life.
T117.5.	Marriage with a tree.
T461.3.	Tree as wife.

26. WOMEN WHO WANT TO BE MEN

Among the Yupa there are some women who want to be men rather than women. They fight like men, and in earlier times they even wore the *manta* of the men.

Once long ago there was a Yupa girl who commenced this curious behavior. Although already full grown, she would accept no husband. The name of this young woman was Uretane. She insisted that she was a man. And her face also looked like that of a man. Soon she even grew a little penis. When she bathed with the women, she went off a little apart from them, being ashamed to bare the lower part of her body before them. She had developed breasts like all the other women.

One day Uretane induced a young woman to go bathe with her. At the river the latter could verify that Uretane had a penis and so she consented to have intercourse with Uretane. Later she related what had happened to all her companions. Finally she fell in love with Uretane, and soon they married, without anyone raising any sort of objection to this relationship. Uretane did all sorts of men's work, and the Yupa of this particular settlement grew accustomed to the pair. It was only occasional guests coming into the village who were somewhat surprised to hear one woman ordering another woman about.*

Summary: *Women Who Want To Be Men*
    Once a woman, who behaves like a man, marries another woman.

Motif Content:	*Women Who Want To Be Men*
F547.2.	Hermaphrodite.
T462.	Lesbian love.

27. THE MAN AND THE DOG

A Yupa had two dogs, one male and one female. But when he went on the hunt he always took along only the bitch, leaving the male dog tied up at home.

On their way through the forest the man conversed with his dog as if she were a woman and then he lay down with her. One day the dog became pregnant and the man was very worried. Luckily, the dog gave birth to her young in the night so that the man could go unseen to kill all six of them. The offspring had been born with human bodies but with dog's heads.

After a certain time the man took the dog on the hunt again. But the latter whined so piteously that the wife suspected and followed them in secret. What she saw on this occasion struck her as so monstrous that she dared not mention it to anyone. But since she had witnessed the doings of her husband, she also knew how it was that the bitch could bear again, and why indeed it was pretended that all of the young had been born dead.

Summary: *The Man and the Dog.*
    A man has intercourse with his dog. He kills the dog's offspring which are half human.

*My informant personally knew of two such cases of transvestites.

Motif Content:	*The Man and the Dog*
B633.	Human and animal offspring from marriage to animal.
T465.	Bestiality.

28. AROKA, THE ANTEATER

In early times there lived a certain woman among the Yupa. One day, as she was going out to get water, she happened to catch and fetter an anteater. She dragged him to the river and hid him in a cave. Each day when she went to the river she misused the beast, by introducing its snout into her vagina. She did this for quite some time until one day she was discovered by her husband. When his wife had gone away he went over, cut the head off the anteater and cooked it. He invited his wife to partake of the game, pretending that he had already eaten his fill while out on the hunt.*

After the meal the woman went again to the river and there she discovered what had happened. She was nauseated; she vomited. When she came back to the settlement, the news had already been broadcast by her husband, and she was driven out of the village. In the meantime this woman must have perished in the forest, all alone.

Summary: *Aroka, the Anteater*

A man who discovers that his wife has sexual relations with an anteater kills the animal and makes her eat its head. She is driven out of the village.

Motif Content:	*Aroka, the Anteater*
G61.+.	Lover's flesh eaten unwittingly. (G61. Relatives' flesh eaten unwittingly.)
Q253.1.	Bestiality punished.
S411.	Wife banished.
T465.	Bestiality.

---

*The Yupa normally discard the heads of all animals killed, because they say that eating heads causes one's hair to turn prematurely gray. According to Bolinder (1958:148) "only the old men would be permitted to eat the head [of deer], for it was believed that the young people would get sick and die if they should eat such meat." See also Santelos 1959-1960:328.

114

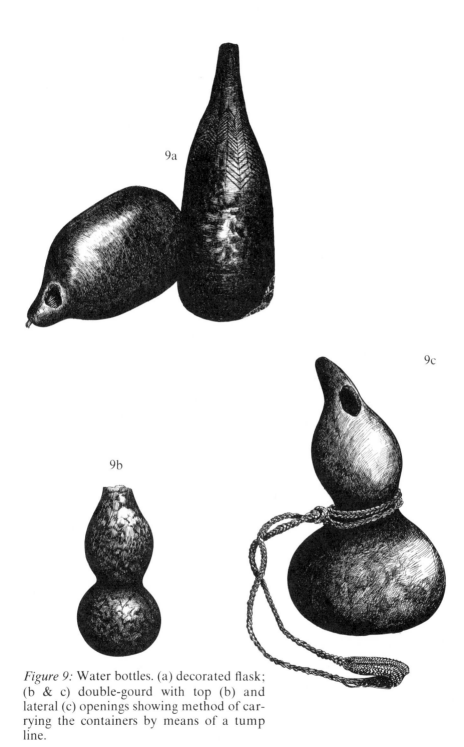

Figure 9: Water bottles. (a) decorated flask; (b & c) double-gourd with top (b) and lateral (c) openings showing method of carrying the containers by means of a tump line.

29. KARAU, THE LORD OF THE ANIMALS

While hunting in the forest a Yupa came upon a great herd of wild boars. He tried to shoot one of them, but it ran between his legs and dragged him to the house of Karau, the Lord of the Animals.

There was a great corral behind the house where all the wild swine lived. Karau led the Yupa there, changed him into a wild boar and placed the whole corral in his charge; he thus became foodmaster and keeper of the swine.

Every day the transformed Yupa took the herd into the forest, climbed on the *guaymaro* trees and shook the fruits down for his new companions.

One day, just as he had shaken down a great store of fruit, the feeding swine were attacked by a band of Yupa, who killed as many as thirty of the animals.

Beside himself with anger the herder of the swine climbed down from the tree shouting murder at the Yupa. "Since I am the father of these beasts, you have killed your own brothers! Don't you dare to eat any of these pigs!"

So the Yupa hunters left the booty for the carrion vulture and went away ashamed. But Karau punished his swineherd by not letting him go back to earth anymore.

Summary: *Karau, the Lord of the Animals*
An Indian transformed into a swine is in charge of a herd of swine. When other Indians attack the herd he scolds them for killing their own brothers.

Motif Content:	*Karau, the Lord of the Animals*
B240.	King of animals.
D136.	Transformation: man to swine.
Q433.	Punishment: imprisonment.

30. THE UNSUCCESSFUL HUNTER

In early times there lived among the Yupa a man who rarely had good luck when out on the hunt. Day after day he went out to hunt *picure;* but he returned time after time having found no meat.

His tribal companions made life a burden to the unsuccessful hunter. Only his wife stayed faithful. She bade him not heed the mockery of the people; he would find his hunting luck again. The man, however, became very silent, until one day he came home with a beaming face. He had found his hunting luck once more, indeed two *picure* had chanced before his arrow! He had already skinned the beasts and now threw them into the cooking pot of his joyful wife.

It happened that on this day the other men had had no luck at all. Most of them returned from the hunt with no meat, and, although they had never given their tribal companion anything during the time when he was forsaken by his hunting luck, he bade his wife distribute a bit of his meat to each of their families. The men felt very ashamed of themselves, but nevertheless they accepted the present.

On the following night the lucky hunter died, and in the early morning all gathered around his body. As they took his *manta* from him to prepare the body for the grave, they discovered to their great surprise that he had bound off both thighs tight with thongs, and had cut away the calves of both his legs. All of them regretted greatly that he had sought to escape their jibes in this manner.

Summary: *The Unsuccessful Hunter*

An unsuccessful hunter tries to escape the mockery of his fellow tribesmen by cutting off his calves and pretending to have killed two animals. He dies.

Motif Content:	*The Unsuccessful Hunter*
K1968.	Sham prowess in hunting (fishing).
N250.	Persistent bad luck.

31. YAMORE, THE DECEIVER

One day the Yupa invited the people from a neighboring tribe to a feast. As the guests arrived, Yamore, the chief of the Yupa, went to greet them. He let them go in front of him, and then he began to grab them by the legs and toss them into the air one after the other. Terrified, they all cried out. But before these cries could reach the ears of their friends, they had already been transformed into birds. Since that day there have been birds, and each different type of bird has its own song.

Summary: *Yamore, the Deceiver*
   A Yupa chief transforms guests from another tribe into birds.

Motif Content:	*Yamore, the Deceiver*
A1900.	Creation of birds.
A2426.2.	Cries of birds.
D150.	Transformation: man to bird.

32. WILD BOARS AND MONKEYS

One day one of the Yupa forefathers made a great number of wooden disks and took them up a high mountain. Once on top, he rolled the disks down the hill and ran after them. When they all reached the foot of the mountain, he ordered them to climb a tree. But this they would not do, and so he changed all of them into wild boars.

After this he made new wooden disks and once again let these roll down the hill. Again he ordered them all to clamber up a tree, and this time it worked. They climbed high up into the top of the tree and were turned into monkeys *(poroto,* black monkey and *shirdi,* white-faced monkey). Ever since, wild boars and these monkeys are found together.

Summary: *Wild Boars and Monkeys*
   An Indian transforms wooden disks into wild boars and monkeys.

Motif Content:	*Wild Boars and Monkeys*
A2493.	Friendships between the animals.
D441.+.	Transformation: wooden disk to animal. (D441. Transformation: vegetable form to animal.)

33. AMUSHA, THE DEER

A Yupa bore a little girl, who cried ceaselessly from the day of her birth. She quieted down and was content only when she was taken out of the house into the open.

One day the mother left the little girl in the house and went into the field. As she returned she began wondering, even while she was some distance from the house, why it was that her child was crying no longer. And when she entered the house, she found it empty. Her daughter had disappeared.

For a long time she searched for the child from house to house. No one had seen her, and only toward evening, as the discouraged mother made her way home, did she find the girl cowering among the roots of a big tree. She picked her up and carried her to the village. She put her on a mat on the ground in front of the house.

As the girl woke up toward morning she marveled that she was once more with her mother, but she stayed and did not run away again. Yet she refused every kind of nourishment that was handed to her. Instead, she ate only *kerehi-, yuruma-,* and *atamara* leaves, which her mother had to bring her each day from the forest. However embarrassed the mother might have been, there was nothing that she could do about it.

And so the girl grew. But to the surprise of her mother, she soon acquired white spots all over her body. Her limbs also changed markedly: the creature no longer ran on two legs as do humans, but on its hands and feet. One day it turned completely into a deer and ran off into the forest, never to return.

Summary: *Amusha, the Deer*
A little girl is afraid of being indoors, and will only eat leaves. When she grows up she turns into a deer.

Motif Content: *Amusha, the Deer*
D114.1.1.2.   Transformation: woman to doe.

34. SANÁYAMŨ, THE SNAKE

A man went out to his field and there he found a beautiful colored snake. Since it was still quite small the man did not want to kill it. He felt sorry for it. Every day he brought it a piece of meat so that it would not be hungry.

After some months the snake had grown very large, and the Yupa had a great deal of trouble to satisfy its burning hunger.

There came a day when fortune on the hunt forsook him, sending him empty-handed to the field to tell the snake. But the snake was angry. She was very hungry, and as she told him this she opened wide her mighty jaws, and falling upon the man, devoured one of his legs.

The Yupa beat her on the head with his bow and was finally able to kill the ravenous beast. But no matter how hard he tried to pull back his leg, he could not. It was some days later before he could tear himself loose. His leg, however, was lost.

Summary: *Sanáyamū, the Snake*
   An Indian who feeds a snake every day has his leg bitten off by the snake when one day he has no food for it.

Motif Content:	*Sanáyamū, the Snake*
K2295.4.+.	Treacherous snake. (K2295.4. Treacherous lizard.)
W154.2.1.	Rescued animal threatens rescuer.

35. KIRIKMÁMARE, THE MOTHER OF SNAKES

Each evening shortly before sunset a woman went to fetch water. But before she actually drew the water she danced for a while to and fro, to and fro.

After she had danced for three weeks in this way, she saw a man coming toward her one evening from the house of the leaf-cutter ants. On each evening thereafter the two embraced each other, until the woman became with child.

Now her husband, who had been away for some time, wanted to meet his wife's lover. Unseen, he followed her to the river one evening. Then he saw Bachaco, this time in the form of a snake, coming toward the woman. He killed the animal just before it came together with his wife. The woman bore many snakes, and thus it came about that the snakes are the children of a human and a leaf-cutter ant.

Summary: *Kirikmámare, the Mother of Snakes*
   A woman has intercourse with a leaf-cutter ant in the form of a man. One day when he appears as a snake her husband kills him. She later gives birth to many snakes.

Motif Content:	*Kirikmámare, the Mother of Snakes*
D382.2.	Transformation: ant to person.
D415.+.	Transformation: insect to snake. (D415. Transformation: insect to another animal.)
T465.	Bestiality.
T554.7.+.	Woman gives birth to snakes. (T554.7. Woman gives birth to a snake.)

36. SARORO, THE OTTER

One day a forefather of the Yupa found a little boy in the woods. His name was Saroro. From the first moment that he laid eyes on him he liked Saroro very much, and took him home where he raised him like one of his own children.

Saroro showed himself to be a very clever boy in all the men's work, especially fishing. Every day he went alone to the river, found little fish under the stones, and ate them up raw. Women, coming to the river to get water, marveled daily at Saroro's skill of catching fish with his bare hand. They begged him to fish for them also, but Saroro had no such desire. He only caught little fish for himself and bigger ones for his family, although he had nothing against his foster-mother giving some of his catch away to other families.

As he grew older, Saroro's skills became perfected. Now he went with his father to the river every day where both caught a great number of fish in a very short time. The other men of the tribe looked with envy on Saroro's great luck at fishing, and although they profited richly from it, they were not well-disposed toward the boy. Who indeed knew where he came from? Who indeed knew who he really was? Perhaps he was the Lord of the Water or the Lord of the Fish himself!

One day Saroro, who had now grown to manhood, proposed that his foster-father build a fish weir and a sturdy house near the river and cease this flighty wandering. The father consented. Shortly after the house was finished a heavy rain set in, but his whole family found the house a safe refuge while they caught a great number of fish both large and small in the weir. Of all the fish, Saroro ate only the *koronchi*, allowing the rest to be divided among the starving and freezing people of the tribe. They filled the roasting grill and were happy indeed to have the diligent Saroro among them.

Soon the rain subsided, and the fish became fewer. But Saroro caught great stocks of fish which supplied not only his own family but also all the other Yupa. Indeed, no matter how hard the other men of the tribe toiled with their hooks, they caught just as good as nothing at all. They became annoyed with Saroro; daily their envy grew. They did not know that it was actually because of him that they had no luck catching fish, and that Saroro had even forbidden the fish to strike at the hooks of the jealous Indians.

It was most discomforting for the foster-father to see his friends turn from him. And so he asked his son to help the other men acquire greater luck in fishing. But Saroro would not consent, although the complaints grew louder and the enemies of his father became more numerous.

During a great feast, at which much *chicha* was drunk, the father hit his foster-son on the head with his bow, so that blood ran over his whole body.

Since this time Saroro has lived no longer among man. He jumped into the water, and has taken all the fish away with him.

Summary: *Saroro, the Otter*

Saroro, a boy adopted by a Yupa family, shows such great skill at fishing that all the other men (whom he has given bad fishing luck) are envious. Finally his foster-father hits him so that he leaves the tribe, taking all the fish with him.

Motif Content:	*Saroro, the Otter*
D682.3.1.	Animals in human form retain animal food and habits.
F660.	Remarkable skill.
K1822.	Animal disguises as human being.
Q281.	Ingratitude punished.
W154.	Ingratitude.
W195.	Envy.

37. PISHICÁRACHA, THE BAT

A man on his way home at night after the hunt heard someone speak to him from inside a hollow tree trunk, inviting him to enter. The hunter went over to the tree and suddenly found himself in the company of bats, who were celebrating a happy holiday there and drinking a great deal of *cashiri*. These invited him to celebrate with them, and the Yupa readily accepted. "We spend each night like this," said the bats as the Yupa took leave. "And you should come regularly, but not without *cashiri.*"

The man had very much enjoyed the frolicsome company of the bats. On another day he bade his wife prepare *cashiri*, which he wanted to take with him on the nightly hunt. On the following evening he poured the brew into several gourds and went to the house of the bats; once more to spend a gay night. Now there was also a young bat-woman there, and so he was loathe to miss even one night at the bat house.

Through the frequent contact with the bats, the Yupa himself slowly began to change into just such a creature. Little nose patches grew on him; he sucked on the clothes of his wife and children; and the children asked their mother one day why their father smelled so of bats. One day the man grew claws. The wife became suspicious. She followed her husband to the house of the bats, from which the *cashiri* flowed. On the following morning the man did not come home at all, and his wife reported to all her people what had happened. She led them to the house of the bats, where she persuaded the men to set fire to the old tree. The sleeping bats were surprised by the flames and fell into the glowing coals at the foot of the tree. The Yupa fell down, last of all; he had the head and claws of a bat, while the rest of his body still retained the form of a human.

Summary: *Pishicáracha, the Bat*

An Indian, who goes every night to visit the bats in their house, begins to turn into a bat. His wife makes the people burn down the bat house, and the Indian and the bats die.

Motif Content:	*Pishicáracha, the Bat*
B299.7.	Festival of animals.
D110.+.	Transformation: man to bat. (D110. Transformation: man to wild beast [mammal].)
D681.	Gradual transformation.
F562.2	Residence in tree.
S112.	Burning to death.

38. PIRI, THE LITTLE STINGING FLIES

One day a woman went into her field to gather yuca. When she got there she felt as if someone were throwing little darts at her back. She went to the edge of the forest which was close by and found there a small clearing where many tiny people were dancing. These took great fright when they became aware of her and tried to hide. But she told them that she was a Yupa and did not wish them any harm.

"We are the *piri*," said the tiny people. "Do not tell your fellow human beings that you have discovered us, lest we fall upon all of you and kill you." The woman quieted the *piri,* but since she had no fear of the threats of the little people, she told all the Yupa what had happened.

Since this day the Yupa have had no more peace. Every day the *piri* swarm over them in great numers and try to kill them. But since the humans have so much blood, the *piri* never succeed. Nevertheless, they are a constant and everlasting plague, and the Yupa flee from them, whenever possible, into the mountains.

Summary: *Piri, the Little Stinging Flies*

A woman breaks her promise not to tell her village about her discovery of the fly people, and since then the flies are a constant plague to the Indians.

Motif Content:	*Piri, the Little Stinging Flies*
A2585.	Why there is enmity between certain animals and man.
M205.	Breaking of bargains or promises.
M244.	Bargains between men and animals.
Q266.	Punishment for breaking promise.

39. THE HUMMINGBIRD KUISHNA

A Yupa woman went one day to her field to gather yuca and baata. As she went about her work all stooped over, she became aware that something had fallen on her back. Gripping it she found that she had a tiny dart in her hand. Although this struck her as curious, for she had not been working under the trees, she continued with her work without attaching much importance to the incident. But it happened again, and then again . . . and now she wanted to get to the bottom of things.

She went to the edge of the forest close by and immediately came across a little clearing. This was wholly laid out with white cotton and in the middle sat Kuishna, the wife of the hummingbird.

"What are you doing there?" asked the Yupa woman. "And why is it that you throw darts at me?"

"I wanted to call you over here," said the hummingbird, "for I wanted to show you something that the Yupa don't know yet.

But remember, you are not allowed to say anything about this to the other women, until you yourself have mastered it perfectly and can do it just as well as I. Look here, I am making cloth from this cotton." At this the Yupa woman laughed aloud and said that all Yupa had been spinning for ages and could weave as well. This was nothing new to her!

"I know that you can spin and weave," replied the humming-bird, "but my kind of cloth is something else entirely. I spread the cotton out in a thick layer and just as large as the cloth should be. Then I bind the various wads and strands together with a few twists and the cloth is ready."

Then the Yupa woman paid close attention and was not a little surprised when the hummingbird completed a big piece of material in a minute or so with very little trouble. Right away she tried to imitate this. But she could not do it. It looked much easier than it really was. She must come again on the morrow, the hummingbird told her, and continue her visits until she had learned it. The woman promised just that and went home.

But once back in the village she could not keep the novelty to herself alone. She gathered all the women around her and whispered to them what had happened. She would show them all, as soon as she had mastered it.

On the next day the woman went again to the hummingbird's clearing. She had not noticed, however, that all the women of the village had followed her there at a distance. As she reached the clearing she found no hummingbird there. The cotton, too, had disappeared. The woman's companions, who by then had caught up with her, laughed her to scorn and called her a liar, although she maintained the opposite.

And thus it was that the Yupa never learned to make cloth in the manner of the hummingbird. They can only spin and weave. The hummingbird never came again. She keeps her secret and carries a few white feathers under each of her wings as a sign of her craft.

Summary: *The Hummingbird Kuishna*

A hummingbird is teaching a woman a very fast way of making cloth from cotton. The woman breaks her promise not to tell the other women. Once, they follow her on her way to the bird but it has disappeared and never comes back.

Motif Content:	*The Hummingbird Kuishna*
B451.+.	Helpful hummingbird. (B451. Helpful birds—passeriformes.)
B561.+.	Animal tells heroine its secret. (B561. Animals tell hero their secrets.)
J130.	Wisdom (knowledge) acquired from animals.
M205.	Breaking of bargains or promises.
M244.	Bargains between men and animals.
Q266.	Punishment for breaking promise.

40. WAHIKU, THE PIPE CLAY

In early times the Yupa prepared only small fields, until one day a powerful *tuano* arose, who mocked them for the size of their fields.

He wanted to show the Yupa how to prepare a real field and so he called the men together to go into the forest with him. There he drew himself up, seized hold of a staff, and stretching it horizontally before him he turned around on the very spot where he stood. Thereupon the trees within a wide circle fell over and burned up. Then the *tuano* turned about once more and sowed the kind of "grass" which the Yupa ate in those days.

When the Yupa came to harvest their field several months later, they saw the big tapir and his companion Wahiku coming. They stood before them and the tapir said: "This field is not good. It is too small!" Then he ran around and around the field urinating on it.

When the Yupa saw that, they tried to stop him. But it was already too late and the field was ruined. The tapir ran around, but his companion Wahiku stayed by the Yupa. Every day he made a number of black and white clay pipes as well as containers of the most varied sort, and although he intended to leave every day he stayed for a long time. Finally, however, expressing his wish to depart, he took his leave. But the Yupa took bows and arrows and shot Wahiku. After his death he was changed into a clay pipe.

The tapir still had two other companions. The *coruba palm* and the *royal palm*. These fled down the mountain together with the tapir. Thus it came to pass the the Yupa in the mountains of the Sierra de Perijá have no tapirs, no *coruba palm* and no *royal palm*, to be sure, but they do have potter's clay for their pipes and containers.

Summary: *Wahiku, the Pipe Clay*

When the Yupa try to prepare one large field instead of many small ones the tapir ruins it, and then flees down the mountain with the *coruba palm* and the *royal palm*. His companion, *Wahiku*, remains to make pipes and containers. On his death at the hands of the Yupa he turns into a clay pipe.

Motif Content:	*Wahiku, the Pipe Clay*
A998.	Origin of clay.
A2434.2.	Why certain animals are absent from countries.
D429.+.	Transformation: animal to clay pipe. (D429. Transformation: animal to object—misc.)
D2157.6.	Field cultivated and sowed by magic.
K344.2.+.	Spoiling field with urine. (K344.2. Spoiling rice field with dung.)

41. THE ORIGIN OF MAIZE

In early times the Yupa possessed no maize. They ate *makáhka* (a tuber which grows in the mountains. It looks somewhat like wild *okumo* and is also just about as sharp.)

One day Oséema, in the form of a small boy, appeared in the village of the Yupa and asked for shelter. The woman of one of the households bade him enter; they invited him to live there, and set *makáhka* before him. The boy, however, did not care for this particular food. Therefore he was constantly scolded when he refused the share apportioned to him.

When Oséema was three years old he stole away into the forest every day to make a calabah full of *túka* for himself. Each time he emptied out the calabash, so that nobody would discover his secret. Although Oséema's foster mother suspected that the boy was feeding himself in some way or other, she never discovered the maize dish he prepared.

As time went on it became rather disagreeable for this family and the others in the village to have the strange lad living among them. They looked not a little askance at him, but as it turned out, particularly because whenever little Oséema urinated various plants sprang up which today we call batata, *auyama,* and bananas. Besides all this, the boy reeked so strongly of these plants that the Yupa drove him out of their village with scoldings and beatings.

Oséema ran into the mountains and there he met his companion Kïrïkï, (Squirrel), who accompanied Oséema on all his journeyings, since he was invisible to mankind for the most part. Oséema related to Kïrïkï all that had befallen him, and together they decided to forsake mankind and earth. Thereupon they made two *atunse* (clarinets) and set out upon their way, making music as they went.

Along their way they happened upon a Yupa village. Three adult women and three girls came running out to meet them, so curious were they about the delightful music. They asked them why they had made these rare instruments and why they made music on them. Oséema explained to them that these were *atunse:* a large one (male) and a little one (female), which he and his companion played as they proceeded on their journey. The women were much taken by the beautiful music and bade the wanderers to tarry a few days. One of the women also offered Oséema her daughter so that his sojourn would be more pleasant. Oséema rejoiced at the confidence of these people, for up to this moment he had experienced nothing but the scoldings and grumblings of mankind, and consented to stay there for a short time with his companion. However, he declined the services of the girl with the excuse that all girls were his true sisters and all women his mothers. So the women urged him no further and were content merely that the two guests stayed on. In the village the women informed their men that far from being strangers both guests were, according to Oséema's own words, their very next-of-kin.

In the evening the men went to hunt, leaving the womenfolk

Figure 10: So-called axe-flute of the Yupa (See Glossary).

behind alone with the two guests. The latter played upon their musical instruments until midnight. Then suddenly Oséema broke off the music and ordered the women and girls to prepare little fields round about their houses. The women, not knowing how to conduct themselves at first, obediently followed the example of Oséema. He showed them everything, and after this work was done he distributed among them kernels of corn which he carried in his head. He asked them to throw these kernels upon the prepared fields. After all kernels had been sown, the women went back to their houses to rest for the remainder of the night after the strenuous work. During the night the maize sprouted, grew high, and ripened. In the fields batata, *auyama,* and bananas were also growing.

The next morning as they stepped out of their houses the women saw what had happened. Oséema bade them be silent and then made himself known to them. He revealed that he had come to earth in order to bring the Yupa a better sustenance than *makáhka.* In the first village, however, he had been mistreated and forced to eat the unpleasant root. It had been in their company that he had first felt comfortable, and in gratitude for their friendship he had made them the gift of the new food plant. From this moment henceforth no *makáhka* should be eaten. Then he showed

Figure 11: Mano and metate for grinding maize meal.

the women and girls how the different crops—but most especially the maize—could be harvested and prepared. The women tasted the maize and then gave some of it to their men, who had returned in the meantime. All found the maize most tasty and gladly forswore *makáhka* for the future. They set themselves straightaway to the task of making new fields, and the women sowed the corn.

A year passed. Oséema and Kïrïkï remained living among the Yupa. News of the strangers and their gifts spread quickly over the mountains, penetrating to the most outlying villages. All the Yupa, even those who had rejected Oséema, begged him for maize. But Oséema did not respond to their pleas and forbade his Yupa friends to give away their maize.*

Oséema and his companion would have stayed with the Yupa for several years more perhaps, had it not been for an unfortunate occurrence. One day a woman had threshed a calabash full of maize and had left it carelessly on a tree trunk which was lying on the ground. Kïrïkï, who was in the process of stepping over the log, hit against the calabash which slid off, scattering the kernels. At this very instant a heavy rain set in, which was a sign to Oséema of what had happened. Because of this Oséema was determined to take his leave of the Yupa. However, he did not punish them further, and even permitted the other Yupa to grow maize after his departure. The Yupa were deeply grieved over the accident as well as the departure of Oséema and attempted to make him change his mind. But Oséema stood by his decision and explicitly forbade the Yupa to make inquiries concerning the destination of his journey.

Following the misfortune, Kïrïkï had hidden himself in the forest, hoping that Oséema would learn nothing of what had happened. But on returning to the village on evening he was told that Oséema had already departed, but whither they did not know, since they had been forbidden to ask his destination.

Kïrïkï knew immediately that he would never find Oséema again. He ran back into the forest, and changed himself into a squirrel.

Soon, however, the rain ceased and all the Yupa began to grow maize. But before they harvest the maize, they blow—even to-

*The Yupa are reluctant to give corn seed to others. They say that seed given to another will thrive and yield excellent crops, whereas that remaining with the donor will fail to produce (Ruddle, personal communication).

130

day—upon the instruments of Oséema, that he may always grant them an abundant new harvest.

Summary: *The Origin of Maize*

Long ago the Yupa had no maize. Oséema seeks shelter as a small boy in a village. Since he does not like the Indian food he secretly eats maize. Finally the Yupa drive him off. With his companion Kïrïkï, he comes to another village where he is treated very well. To reward the people he teaches them how to plant maize and other plants. One day Kïrïkï accidentally upsets a bowl of maize and because of this Oséema leaves the village forever.

Motif Content:	*The Origin of Maize*
A541.	Culture hero teaches arts and crafts.
A560.	Culture hero's (demigod's) departure.
A2611.0.5.	Parts of human or animal body transformed into plants.
A2685.1.1.	Origin of maize.
A2687.5.	Origin of banana.
D117.	Transformation: man to rodent.
D646.2.	Transformation to child or pet to be adopted.
D1002.1.	Magic urine.
D2157.2.	Magic quick growth of crops.
F687.	Remarkable fragrance (odor) of person.
J1732.	Ignorance of certain foods.
N300.	Unlucky accidents.
Q1.	Hospitality rewarded—opposite punished.
Z235.	Hero with extraordinary animal companions.

42. THE ORIGIN OF TUBERS*

In early times the Yupa did not know of yuca and *batata*. They lived off the animals in the forest—wild boar they liked to eat best.

One day the men left the village to go out hunting for wild boars. They surrounded a great number and drove them all together with loud shouts. Luck was with them and they made a rich haul. They bundled up the animals and went on home. Nobody noticed that one of their companions was missing.

*See also narrative 7 and the note to narrative 2.

131

During the drive, this man had lost himself in the wooded hills and had wandered in wide circles all day long. He tried in vain to communicate with his friends; beating upon the roots of the trees with his bow, and shouting their names. Nobody could hear him. He ran on, further and further, even though it was already dark, for he did not want to give up. But his path grew worse in the darkness: he crashed into the trees, tripped, and suddenly— he fell into the net trap of the tiger people! Try as he might, he could not free himself from this net. So he waited in great fear for the tiger, which would come by dawn's first light to check his trap.

Even before the sun had risen the Indian heard the hungry sounds of the approaching tiger. Suddenly there he was standing over him! It was not the old tiger himself who had come—but his son. Tiger-Son saw the shivering Indian, tore open the netting of the trap and let the man escape before Tiger-Father came to eat him up.

The Yupa ran fast, as fast as he could. It began to rain. Once he turned in his fear to make sure that the great tiger was not following him. To his great surprise he saw all the rain water flowing together behind him so that it towered up into a wave tree-high! In his fear he ran faster and faster to get nearer to the sun—for it seemed that the closer he came to sun, the further behind remained the wave. Soon he stood directly beneath the sun, and there he noticed a boy who was gazing up at the sun, speaking with him.

The lad was the son of the moon. He had been sent out by his father to pick up a bird from Sun, his uncle. Sun, the brother of Moon, is a very fine hunter.

"Uncle! Throw me down a few good birds!" the boy called to Sun. But Sun lied to him, saying that he had none but a few small bony ones, which he would throw down to him. Saying this, he stuffed the plumpest bird into his own mouth, for he wanted to see his nephew leave quite empty-handed.

As the boy saw the Indian running past, he told him he should rather hide himself, or better yet, quit the site altogether and quickly too, so that his uncle would not see him. "Sun," he said, "loves the taste of human flesh!"

But Sun had already seen the Yupa.

"I am coming down!" he called to the boy. "I'll catch a great

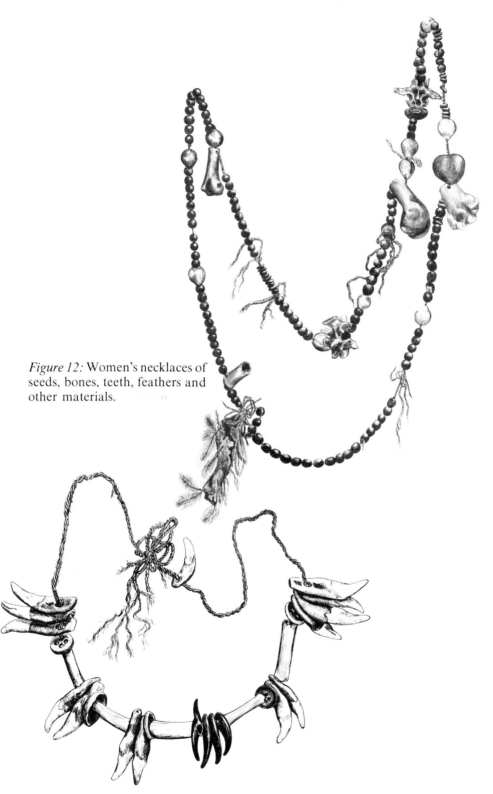

Figure 12: Women's necklaces of seeds, bones, teeth, feathers and other materials.

133

big bird just for you! But do not look up at me for your eyes will be burned. And you know what a hot behind I have!"

So Sun came down from the heavens, and instead of giving the boy the bird he had promised him, he seized the Yupa and drew him close. "The man belongs to me!" objected the lad. "I found him first!" But Sun only laughed in his face and ordered him to go home.

The son of Moon ran to his father as fast as he could and told him all that had happened—how his uncle had lied to him and thrown no birds down at all, and how in the end he had taken captive the Yupa, who certainly would die, unless Moon came to his aid.

So then Moon determined to save the man. He hurried to the house of his brother. He saw that Sun had already prepared much tobacco juice to give to the human. After he drank this the Yupa would be heavily drugged and could then be eaten. But the Indian had refused to drink so very much tobacco juice. Moon took the calabash from the hand of Sun and drank until it was empty.

"I am taking the man along with me," said Moon to Sun. "You will get him back later on." So Moon, his son, and the Yupa left Sun, who swore to come to the house of Moon to get the man some time before evening.

Moon hid the Yupa away in the cave where the young girls are brought to spend the days of their first menstruation. Toward evening Sun came, but only as far as the entrance, not daring to go into the cave, for it is forbidden for men to see girls in this condition. So he went away again complaining angrily.

Moon has a very big family—one wife, very many daughters, but only one son. Sun is lord of a huge group—the stars. But Sun has no family of his own and he and his brother Moon are on very poor terms with one another.

So the Yupa Indian passed two months in the cave of the moon-daughters. Moon's wife brought him food. Nights he was allowed to leave the cave because Sun slept then and could not watch the opening.

One evening Moon came to the cave and asked the Yupa to tell him all about mankind.

The story of the life and the customs of men impressed Moon so much that he took great pride in having such a guest and even offered the Yupa one of his daughters in marriage. He also said that the Indian might have sexual relations with his other daughters.

Although the Yupa lacked nothing, he found life in the company of the moon people rather boring. Forced to sleep all day long and being able to leave the cave only at night in time became a torment to the man.

And so he went to Moon and asked for permission to return to his own people. Moon was full of understanding and agreed.

As a gift to human beings on earth he gave the Yupa some yuca roots and batata, telling him how to plant and harvest them. On the following night the Yupa said goodbye to the moon family—to moon wife, to moon daughters, to the son of Moon, and to Moon himself.

Again he felt the cold of Moon, as he had always felt it when he talked with him and when, at night, the behind of Moon lit the dark of heaven and of earth. "Take care," said Moon in parting from him, "that you take no warm food on earth, and above all do not drink hot *chicha,* or you will die, for you have been in our land too long!"

After a long, long journey the Yupa found himself in his own village once more. He showed the Indians the gifts he received from Moon and told them how the plants are planted, harvested, and enjoyed. All batata and yuca plants stem from these first tubers.

But the Yupa to whom Moon had given these gifts died very soon after his return. He was cold all the time, and one day he could stand it no longer. He took a calabash of quite warm *chicha,* drank it down, fell over, and was dead.

Summary: *The Origin of Tubers*

A Yupa, who gets lost during a hunting trip, is caught by the sun who wants to eat him. He is saved by the moon and taken to live with the moon's family, where he marries one of the moon's daughters. Finally he gets tired of their nocturnal existence and asks to return to his own people. The moon gives him yuca roots and batata (hitherto unknown to the Indians) when he leaves. Soon after his return he dies from drinking warm *chicha,* as a consequence of his disobedience to the moon's instructions.

Motif Content:	*The Origin of Tubers*
A711.2.	Sun as a cannibal.
A736.3.	Sun and moon as brothers.
A738.2.	Mental powers and disposition of sun.
A745.	Family of the moon.
A753.2.	Moon has house.
A753.3.1.	Moon deceives sun.
A753.3.4.	Moon endowed with wisdom and passion.
A764.1.	Stars as children of the moon.
A1423.4.	Acquisition of manioc.
A1441.	Acquisition of agriculture.
B545.+.	Tiger rescues man from trap (net). (B545. Animal rescues from trap [net].)
C141.	Tabu: going forth during menses.
D2151.0.3.	Wall of water magically warded off.
F16.	Visit to land of moon.
F164.	Habitable caves and mounds in otherworld.
J652.	Inattention to warnings.
N771.+.	Man lost on hunt has adventures. (N771. King [prince] lost on hunt has adventures.)

43. ARARE, THE TAPIR

A woman who had married very young had just born her first baby. Soon after the birth of the child the father went into the forest to prepare a small field. He felled the trees and burned the dried wood. Then he sent out his wife, who was to sow corn on the field.

For several days the woman went to the field to do what she had been ordered. But evenings when her husband asked her whether she had finished she constantly replied that there was still one piece to do.

The Yupa knew, of course, that he had cleared only a very small piece of forest for the field, and he could not believe that his wife needed so much time to sow it. Since he wanted to find out the real reason for the delay, he followed her secretly to the field the very next day.

How surprised he was to see that his little field had grown enormously. Suddenly he saw how his wife changed herself into a tapir, at the same time changing the child on her back into

136

a big hump. The tapir ate the young plants which had shot up with juicy shoots out of the burned-off field. While the animal slowly went forward, the forest yielded before it and was transformed into a new piece of field. The tapir would have felled the entire forest in this manner had not the man interfered and asked her to stop. "Go! Eat the fruit of the *coruba*, eat *sapera!*" he shouted at his transformed wife. Seized with fear the latter took flight, through the river, and through rapids, downwards, always down river, never to return.

Summary: *Arare, the Tapir*

A man sees his wife, transformed into a tapir, eat all the plants on his field instead of sowing. He promptly chases her down the mountain.

Motif Content:	*Arare, the Tapir*
D110.+.	Transformation: woman to tapir (D110. Transformation: man to wild beast [mammal].)
D451.1.+.	Transformation: trees to field. (D451.1. Transformation: tree to other object.)
K2213.	Treacherous wife.
Q556.	Curse as punishment.

44. KARAU, THE SPIRIT OF THE NIGHT

A Yupa girl, menstruating for the first time in her life, was once passing the time away in a little hut high in the mountains. To her great surprise she was visited one night by someone whose body was covered all over with hair, whose teeth were very, very large, and whose hands were very cold indeed. He slept with the girl and then he disappeared again.

On the next day the maiden told her mother what had happened. The mother said that it had been Karau. The girl became very fearful of spending the coming night alone, but the mother told her to make a good fire. Karau is afraid of fire.

So the mother left her daughter. When she came back to the hut on the next day she found only the head of the girl. Karau had devoured her.

The Yupa then went out to look for Karau and did not rest until they finally found him in a dark and gloomy thicket. They killed him, spitted his body on a pole, and burned him.

Summary: *Karau, the Spirit of the Night*

A young girl, isolated during her menstruation, is devoured by Karau, the night spirit.

Motif Content:	*Karau, the Spirit of the Night*
C142.	Tabu: sexual intercourse during menses.
F401.5.	Spirits appear horrible.
F402.1.11.2.	Evil spirit kills and eats person.
F420.6.1.7. + .	Night spirit surprises and rapes mortal woman. (F420.6.1.7. Water spirit surprises and rapes mortal woman.)
F470.	Night spirits.
S139.2.2.1. + .	Head of spirit impaled upon stake. (S139.2.2.1. Heads of slain enemies impaled upon stakes.)

45. KARAU, THE HUNTER

A man had two wives and two daughters. One day he went out to hunt. Night fell and still he did not return. Finally, toward midnight, the women heard someone coming—panting as he came, as if under a heavy load. They ran over there and saw a man dragging his booty along toward the camp. The women helped. Then they went to work right away to ready a big piece of meat.

As the fire blazed high the man turned his back to the women and girls, saying that the light hurt his eyes. The wives did not think this strange, but the man's appearance struck the children as funny. They did not think the man was their father, and in whispers to their mothers asked if they had seen his long finger-nails, his beard, and all that long hair.

But the women paid no attention to the children. They ate, and did not object when the man asked for sexual favors.

Toward midnight, the night-hunter sat up, took a piece of meat, and disappeared into the darkness.

Of course the children were right. It was not their father, but Karau, who had taken advantage of the husband's absence to approach the women. The truth came out when the man returned the next morning.

Summary: *Karau, the Hunter*

While a man is out hunting, Karau, pretending to be the husband, has intercourse with his wives.

Motif Content:	*Karau, the Hunter*
D658.2.	Transformation to husband's (lover's) form to seduce woman.
F401.	Appearance of spirits.
F402.1.4. +.	Spirit assumes human form in order to deceive. (F402.1.4. Demons assume human forms in order to deceive.)
H50.	Recognition by bodily marks or physical attributes.
J652.	Inattention to warnings.

46. MASHÍRAMŨ, THE BUSH SPIRIT

The bush spirit Mashiramū appeared one day in the land of the Yupa and killed many men and many animals. The Yupa greatly feared this demon, for his whole body was covered with much hair and his feet were turned around backwards.

Finally, the Yupa determined to fight Mashiramū. They killed many tigritos, tigers and pumas. Then came Mashiramū with many big tigers and killed all the Yupa. Few remained alive. And even today, humans and tigers battle to the death whenever they come across one another.

Motif Content:	*Mashíramũ, the Bush Spirit*
A2585. +.	Why there is enmity between tigers and man. (A2585. Why there is enmity between certain animals and man.)
F401.5.	Spirits appear horrible.
F401.9.	Spirit with feet turned wrong way.
F402.1.12.	Spirit fights against person.
F441.	Wood spirit.
G346.2.	Devastating demon.

47. OPI, THE SPIRITS OF THE NIGHT

One night an *opi* went into a village with his nephew to abduct a Yupa. They went by the sleeping people one by one, feeling the nose of each, and in this fashion they sought out an old man whom they stuffed into a large carrying basket and took off into the forest. On the way the nephew begged his uncle to let him have the testicles of the man. But the uncle scolded him soundly and told him to be silent lest the old man in the basket wake up. But the prisoner had already awakened because of the whistling noises around him (*opi*, you see, converse by whistling). He jumped from the basket and fled.

But the night spirits followed the old man. Like dogs, they picked up the scent of his track, and thus came to a house where there were a great number of old people asleep. But this time the elder of the night spirits went alone into the house, so that the younger would not drive away the quarry a second time. He chose an old person for himself, grabbed him by the ankle bone, and flung him against the prickly trunk of a palm tree in the forest.

The night spirits kill many people in this fashion. One does well to keep a fire, should their whistling be heard anywhere near the camp.

Summary: *Opi, the Spirits of the Night*

The *opi* abduct an old man at night. When the prisoner flees they return to the village, grab another old man, and kill him. Moral: One does well to keep a fire.

Motif Content:	*Opi, the Spirits of the Night*
F262.7. +.	Spirits whistle. (F262.7. Fairies whistle.)
F402.1.10.	Spirit pursues person.
F402.1.11.	Spirit causes death.
F405.	Means of combating spirits.
F470.	Night spirits.
G302.9.2. +.	Demons abduct man. (G302.9.2. Demons abduct men and torment them.)
G441.	Ogre carries victim in bag (basket).

Tale Fragments

48. THE HOUSE OF THE MOON

The house of the moon is not made of wood, but out of snakes.

Tragavenados serve as posts, *macaurel* as rafters and *jorungaculo (culebra de dos cabezas, cusha)* as ledge beams. The smaller kinds of snakes are the binding material, although in tying fast the beams only their tails are used. If someone goes by this house, these smaller snakes leap at him and hit him with their heads, but to bite they are not able.

Motif Content:	*The House of the Moon*
A753.2.	Moon has house.
F771.1.+.	House made of snakes. (F771.1. Castle of unusual material.)

49. CHIKIMO

High in the hills, deep in the tribal territory of the Irapa, is a rugged crag known as Chikimo. It is shunned by all the Yupa, for in its many caves are hidden terrifying secrets. Once a hunter venturing too near to the foot of this crag was suddenly transformed into a monkey—being quite unaware of what had happened! Were he to shoot an animal, it too would be transformed—in this case into a leaf. Shortly thereafter the hunter was smitten by an intense headache and died.

Belonging to the many sinister inhabitants dwelling in this rocky crag is a kind of a snake *(wán)*, which pursues everybody it sees. In chasing a fleeing man, these snakes inflate the front portion of the body until they can actually fly. No matter how far the beleaguered man may run, the snakes pursue him relentlessly until they finally reach the exhausted victim and kill him with one bite.

The owner of this great rock, which looks like a white house with many windows in it, is Peshewiipi, the lord of all the animals. He appeared as a man to the first human being (who dared to venture into the vicinity of his home), then suddenly changed himself into a frightful storm. And the game which the hunter was fixing over a fire was transformed into wind and disappeared into the flames. At the foot of the mountain stands a great dome-shaped tree, bearing juicy green leaves, which are all poisonous. All animals which feed on its leaves or on its fruit immediately fall over and die. This explains the enormous heap of weathered bones which are to be seen under the tree. Forever guarding this mountain is a gigantic eagle called Seremo.

Motif Content:	*Chikimo*
A418.+.	Lord of particular mountain. (A418. Deity of particular mountain.)
B240.	King of animals.
B455.3.	Helpful eagle.
D118.2.	Transformation: man (woman) to monkey.
D281.	Transformation: man to storm.
D932.	Magic mountain.
D2060.	Death or bodily injury by magic.
F771.5.1.+.	Magic mountain guarded by eagle. (F771.5.1. Castle guarded by beasts.)
F811.7.	Tree with extraordinary fruit.
F1021.+.	Extraordinary flights through air by snake. (F1021. Extraordinary flights through air.)

50. ADVICE FOR HUNTERS

If a man kills many animals and is unable to eat them all, the Lord of Birds appears and devours this man.

If a man has killed many wild pigs and roasted their meat to preserve it, he must take a piece thereof, sprinkle it with red powder, and put it at the entrance of the village for Karau.

If a man has shot many birds, he must stick a bush knife in the middle of the path for the Lord of the Birds. He will take this, and, being reconciled with the hunter, will not come into the village.

Motif Content:	*Advice for Hunters*
B242.	King of birds
F406.	Spirits propitiated.

51. THE TAPIRS

A Yupa married, and allowed his wife to work a field which he had prepared. But she did not wish to and would do no work. And so, at the command of a spirit, he drove her away into the forest, where she turned herself into a tapir. All tapirs stem from her.

Motif Content:	*The Tapirs*
A1889.1. +.	Origin of tapir. (A1889,1. Creation of tapir.)
D110. +.	Transformation: woman to tapir. (D110. Transformation: man to wild beast [mammal].)
Q321.	Laziness punished.
W111.3.	The lazy wife.

52. WILD BOARS

A Yupa cut a forked branch from a tree and between its prongs he fixed an ax with a wooden disk. He ran so fast downhill with this implement that he changed into a wild boar. From his stem all animals of this species.

Motif Content:	*Wild Boars*
A1871.1.	Origin of wild boar.

53. SNAKES

God prepared a calabash full of poison and emptied it out on the earth. The humans who were supposed to have caught it, neglected to do so, and so snakes came and licked it up, obtaining their poison in this way. Then they fled into the forest ahead of the Yupa, who wanted to kill them. From that time forward snakes have been enemies of mankind.

Motif Content:	*Snakes*
A2532.1.	Why snakes are venomous.
A2585. +.	Why there is enmity between snakes and man. (A2585. Why there is enmity between certain animals and man.)

54. TREES

Formerly most trees were human beings. But these soon split into two groups which quarrelled—for the one did not wish to let the other live in the plains. After a long struggle both groups gave up and the mountain trees let those in the plains live in peace.

Motif Content:	*Trees*
A2282. +.	Present habitat of trees result of ancient quarrel. (A2282. Present habitat of animals result of ancient quarrel.)
D215.	Transformation: man to tree.

III: Motif Distribution
and Indices

Motif Distribution by Motif Groups

According to the following motif inventory, Yupa folk literature indicates three major motif groups: MYTHOLOGICAL MOTIFS (72 = 23%), MARVELS (59 = 19%), and MAGIC (40 = 13%). Motif frequency decreases abruptly in the subsequent cluster of the next four motif groups: REWARDS AND PUNISHMENTS (21 = 6%), DECEPTIONS (20 = 6%), ANIMALS, and SEX (each 15 = 4%). Remaining motif groups each contain so few motifs as to be statistically unimportant. It is interesting to note that in a similar study undertaken of Warao folk literature the three major motif groups coincide with those in the present collection, although the percentage figures differ. In both cases the subsequent clusters of three or four motif groups also largely coincide, with the exception of the category SEX which occupies a more prominent place in Yupa folk literature (Wilbert, 1970:28–32).

As for the motif subgroups, the one most prevalent is by far *marvelous creatures*—as in the case of the Warao—occurring 34 times (11%) in 14 (25%) of the narratives. Also prevalent are *transformation* which occurs 22 times (7%) in 16 (29%) narratives, *cosmogony and cosmology* 20 times (6%) in 5 (9%) narratives, *creation and ordering of human life* 17 times (5%) in 7 (12%) narratives and *otherworld journeys* 16 times (5%) in 4 (7%) narratives.

MOTIF GROUP	MOTIF SUBGROUP	NO. OF MOTIFS
MYTHOLOGICAL MOTIFS	Cosmogony and cosmology	20
	Creation and ordering of human life	17
	Animal characteristics	9
	World calamities	8
	Origin of trees and plants	6
	Demigods and culture heroes	4
	Creation of animal life	3
	Gods	2
	Creator	1
	Topographical features of the earth	1
	Establishment of natural order	1
	Subtotal motifs	72

MOTIF GROUP	MOTIF SUBGROUP	NO. OF MOTIFS
MARVELS	Marvelous creatures	34
	Otherworld journeys	16
	Extraordinary places and things	6
	Extraordinary occurrences	3
	Subtotal motifs	59
MAGIC	Transformation	22
	Magic persons and manifestations	13
	Magic objects	5
	Subtotal motifs	40
REWARDS AND PUNISHMENTS	Kinds of punishment	12
	Deeds punished	8
	Deeds rewarded	1
	Subtotal motifs	21
DECEPTIONS	Villains and traitors	7
	Capture by deception	2
	Fatal deception	2
	Seduction or deceptive marriage	2
	Deception through shams	2
	Deceptive bargains	1
	Thefts and cheats	1
	Escape by deception	1
	Deception into self-injury	1
	False accusations	1
	Subtotal motifs	20
ANIMALS	Friendly animals	6
	Animals with human traits	4
	Fanciful traits of animals	2
	Mythical animals	1
	Magic animals	1
	Marriage of person to animal	1
	Subtotal motifs	15
SEX	Illicit sexual relations	8
	Conception and birth	3
	Marriage	2
	Married life	2
	Subtotal motifs	15

MOTIF GROUP	MOTIF SUBGROUP	NO. OF MOTIFS
TABU	Sex tabu	8
	Speaking tabu	1
	Subtotal motifs	9
UNNATURAL CRUELTY	Revolting murders or mutilations	5
	Cruel relatives	3
	Cruel persecutions	1
	Subtotal motifs	9
THE DEAD	Ghosts and other revenants	6
	Resuscitation	1
	Subtotal motifs	7
CHANCE AND FATE	Accidental encounters	3
	Unlucky accidents	2
	The ways of luck and fate	1
	Helpers	1
	Subtotal motifs	7
THE WISE AND THE FOOLISH	Wise and unwise conduct	3
	Fools (and other unwise persons)	2
	Acquisition and possession of wisdom (knowledge)	1
	Subtotal motifs	6
TRAITS OF CHARACTER	Unfavorable traits of character	6
	Subtotal motifs	6
OGRES	Kinds of ogres	4
	Falling into ogre's power	1
	Subtotal motifs	5
TESTS	Identity tests: recognition	1
	Tests of prowess: tasks	1
	Tests of prowess: quests	1
	Other tests	1
	Subtotal motifs	4
ORDAINING THE FUTURE	Bargains and promises	4
	Subtotal motifs	4

MOTIF GROUP	MOTIF SUBGROUP	NO. OF MOTIFS
CAPTIVES AND FUGITIVES	Captivity	1
	Rescues	1
	Subtotal motifs	2
RELIGION	Religious beliefs	1
	Subtotal motifs	1
MISC. GROUPS OF MOTIFS	Heroes	1
	Subtotal motifs	1
TOTAL: 19	67	303

Motif Distribution by Narrative

A. MYTHOLOGICAL MOTIFS

    a. Creator (A32.3.) 1
    b. Gods (A141.1.+.–A418.+.) 1, 49
    c. Demigods and culture heroes (A526.7.–A560.) 1, 13, 41
    d. Cosmogony and cosmology (A711.2.–A812.) 2, 3, 7, 42, 48
    e. Topographical features of the earth (A998.) 40
    f. World calamities (A1006.1.+.–A1068.+.) 2, 3, 15
    g. Establishment of natural order (A1170.) 2
    h. Creation and ordering of human life (A1252.–A1620.) 1, 5, 7, 10. 13, 15, 42
    j. Creation of animal life (A1871.1.–A1900.) 31, 51, 52
    k. Animal characteristics (A2282.+.–A2585.+.) 3, 31, 32, 38, 40, 46, 53, 54
    l. Origin of trees and plants (A2611.0.5.–A2687.5.) 7, 41

B. ANIMALS

    a. Mythical animals (B16.6.5.) 23
    b. Magic animals (B151.) 6
    c. Animals with human traits (B240.–B299.7.) 29, 37, 49, 50
    d. Friendly animals (B451.+.–B561.+.) 1, 10, 39, 42, 49
    e. Marriage of person to animal (B633.) 27
    f. Fanciful traits of animals (B784.1.) 22, 23

C. TABU

    a. Sex tabu (C112.–C145.+.) 5, 6, 15, 17, 22, 42, 44
    b. Speaking tabu (C423.3.) 6

D. MAGIC

    a. Transformation (D110.+.–D682.3.1.) 2, 25, 29, 31, 32, 33, 35, 36, 37, 40, 41, 43, 45, 49, 51, 54
    b. Magic objects (D932.–D1402.19.) 9, 17, 41, 49
    c. Magic persons and manifestations (D1810.8.3.1.–D2162.) 4, 9, 10, 13, 15, 20, 40, 41, 42, 49

E. THE DEAD

    a. Resuscitation (E151.) 15
    b. Ghosts and other revenants (E310.–E752.5.+.) 6, 18

F. MARVELS

    a. Otherworld journeys (F16.–F183.+.) 6, 7, 8, 42
    b. Marvelous creatures (F262.7.+.–F687.) 8, 11, 14, 16, 23, 26, 36, 37, 41, 44, 45, 46, 47, 50
    c. Extraordinary places and things (F771.1.+.–F811.20.) 1, 10, 12, 48, 49
    d. Extraordinary occurrences (F943.1.+.–F1021.+.) 12, 15, 49

G. OGRES

    a. Kinds of ogres (G61.+.–G346.2.) 11, 28, 46, 47
    b. Falling into ogre's power (G441.) 47

H. TESTS

    a. Identity tests: recognition (H50.) 45
    b. Tests of prowess: tasks (H976.) 5
    c. Tests of prowess: quests (H1250.1.) 6
    d. Other tests (H1569.) 6

J. THE WISE AND THE FOOLISH

    a. Acquisition and possession of wisdom (knowledge) (J130.) 39
    b. Wise and unwise conduct (J652.–J670.) 14, 42, 45
    c. Fools (and other unwise persons) (J1732.–J1919.) 8, 41

K. DECEPTIONS

    a. Deceptive bargains (K194.+.) 15
    b. Thefts and cheats (K344.2.+.) 40
    c. Escape by deception (K500.) 14
    d. Capture by deception (K710.–K778.1.) 10, 14
    e. Fatal deception (K834.+.–K951.0.1.+.) 9, 11
    f. Deception into self-injury (K1113.+.) 10
    g. Seduction or deceptive marriage (K1326.–K1326.+.) 17, 24
    h. Deception through shams (K1822.–K1968.) 30, 36
    j. False accusations (K2100.) 18
    k. Villains and traitors (K2212.0.1.+.–K2295.4.+.) 9, 11, 16, 21, 24, 34, 43

M. ORDAINING THE FUTURE

    a. Bargains and promises (M205.–M244.) 38, 39

N. CHANCE AND FATE

    a. The ways of luck and fate (N250.) 30
    b. Unlucky accidents (N300.–N350.+.) 7, 41
    c. Accidental encounters (N741.–N771.+.) 6, 7, 42
    d. Helpers (N810.4.) 10

Q. REWARDS AND PUNISHMENTS

    a. Deeds rewarded (Q1.) 41
    b. Deeds punished (Q211.8.–Q321.) 9, 19, 21, 28, 36, 38, 39, 51
    c. Kinds of punishment (Q411.–Q556.) 2, 11, 13, 15, 18, 19, 20, 21, 22, 29, 43

R. CAPTIVES AND FUGITIVES

    a. Captivity (R39.+.) 4
    b. Rescues (R111.6.) 10

S. UNNATURAL CRUELTY

    a. Cruel relatives (S62.–S74.1.+.) 17, 21

    b. Revolting murders or mutilations (S111.–S139.2.2.1.+.) 9, 17, 21, 37, 44

    c. Cruel persecutions (S411.) 28

T. SEX

    a. Marriage (T111.5.–T117.5.) 8, 25

    b. Married life (T211.9.–T288.) 10, 17

    c. Illicit sexual relations (T410.+.–T465.) 17, 18, 24, 25, 26, 27, 28, 35

    d. Conception and birth (T523.+.–T554.7.+.) 10, 35

V. RELIGION

    a. Religious beliefs (V311.) 1

W. TRAITS OF CHARACTER

    a. Unfavorable traits of character (W111.3.–W195.) 6, 19, 34, 36, 51

Z. MISC. GROUPS OF MOTIFS

    a. Heroes (Z235.) 41

The Topical Motif Index

A. MYTHOLOGICAL MOTIFS

    a. Creator A32.3.

A32.3.	*Creator's wife.* (1)

    b. Gods A141.1.+.−A418.+.

A141.1.+.	*God makes wooden images and vivifies them.* (*A141.1. God makes automata and vivifies them.*) (1)
A418.+.	*Lord of particular mountain.* (*A418. Deity of particular mountain.*) (49)

    c. Demigods and culture heroes A526.7.−A560.

A526.7.	*Culture hero performs remarkable feats of strength and skill.* (13)
A541.	*Culture hero teaches arts and crafts.* (41)
A545.	*Culture hero establishes customs.* (1)
A560.	*Culture hero's (demigod's) departure.* (41)

    d. Cosmogony and cosmology A711.2.−A812.

A711.2.	*Sun as a cannibal.* (7); (42)
A711.3.+.	*Originally two suns but no moon.* (*A711.3. Originally a moon but no sun.*) (2)
A736.3.	*Sun and moon as brothers.* (2); (42)
A736.3.3.	*Sun and his brother rise and set alternately.* (2)
A738.2.	*Mental powers and disposition of sun.* (42)
A740.	*Creation of the moon.* (2)
A745.	*Family of the moon.* (2); (42)
A753.2.	*Moon has house.* (42); (48)
A753.3.1.	*Moon deceives sun.* (42)
A753.3.4.	*Moon endowed with wisdom and passion.* (42)
A755.6.	*Moon's phases as punishment for moon's misdoing.* (2)
A759.3.	*Why the moon is pale.* (2)
A764.1.	*Stars as children of the moon.* (42)
A764.1.+.	*Moon's son is a star.* (*A764.1. Stars as children of the moon.*) (2)
A778.	*Origin of the Milky Way.* (2)
A812.	*Earth diver.* (3)

    e. Topographical features of the earth A998.

A998.	*Origin of clay.* (40)

    f. World calamities A1006.1.+.−A1068.+.

A1006.1.+.	*New race from single pair (or several) after tribal calamity.* (*A1006.1. New race from single pair [or several] after world calamity.*) (15)

154

	A1009.+.	*Flood.* (A1009. *World catastrophes—misc.*) (3)
	A1010.1.	*Sun does not shine during deluge.* (15)
	A1018.1.	*Flood as punishment for breaking tabu.* (15)
	A1018.2.	*Flood as punishment for incest.* (15)
	A1022.	*Escape from deluge on mountain.* (3)
	A1028.	*Bringing deluge to end.* (15)
	A1068.+.	*Sun thrown on fire.* (A1068. *Sun thrown on fire: period of darkness, rain.*) (2)
g.	Establishment of natural order A1170.	
	A1170.	*Origin of night and day.* (2)
h.	Creation and ordering of human life A1252.–A1620.	
	A1252.	*Creation of man from wood.* (1)
	A1252.1.	*Mankind from vivified wooden image.* (1)
	A1271.	*Origin of first parents.* (1)
	A1273.1.	*Incestuous first parents.* (1)
	A1337.	*Origin of disease.* (15)
	A1337.0.2.+.	*Disease caused by evil spirit.* (A1337.0.2. *Disease caused by ghosts.*) (15)
	A1414.4.	*Origin of fire—gift from god.* (5)
	A1414.5.	*Origin of flint and tinder.* (5)
	A1423.4.	*Acquisition of manioc.* (7); (42)
	A1426.2.1.	*Introduction of brewing.* (1)
	A1441.	*Acquisition of agriculture.* (42)
	A1459.1.+.	*Origin of white man's weapons.* (1459.1. *Acquisition of weapons.*) (10)
	A1552.1.	*Why brothers and sisters do not marry.* (1)
	A1552.3.	*Brother-sister marriage of children of first parents.* (1)
	A1614.9.	*Origin of white man.* (10)
	A1620.	*Distribution of tribes.* (13)
j.	Creation of animal life A1871.1.–A1900.	
	A1871.1.	*Origin of wild boar.* (52)
	A1889.1.+.	*Origin of tapir.* (A1889.1. *Creation of tapir.*) (51)
	A1900.	*Creation of birds.* (31)
k.	Animal characteristics A2282.+.–A2585.+.	
	A2282.+.	*Present habitat of trees result of ancient quarrel.* (A2282. *Present habitat of animals result of ancient quarrel.*) (54)
	A2291.+.	*Animal characteristics acquired during flood.* (A2291. *Animal characteristics obtained during deluge.*) (3)
	A2426.2.	*Cries of birds.* (31)
	A2434.2.	*Why certain animals are absent from countries.* (40)
	A2493.	*Friendships between the animals.* (32)

A2532.1.	*Why snakes are venomous.* (53)
A2585.	*Why there is enmity between certain animals and man.* (38)
A2585.+.	*Why there is enmity between tigers and man.* (A2585. *Why there is enmity between certain animals and man.*) (46)
A2585.+.	*Why there is enmity between snakes and man.* (A2585. *Why there is enmity between certain animals and man.*) (53)

l. Origin of trees and plants A2611.0.5.–A2687.5.

A2611.0.5.	*Parts of human or animal body transformed into plants.* (41)
A2684.3.	*Origin of cotton plant.* (7)
A2685.1.1.	*Origin of maize.* (41)
A2686.4.3.	*Origin of yams.* (7)
A2687.5.	*Origin of banana.* (7); (41)

B. ANIMALS

a. Mythical animals B16.6.5.

| B16.6.5. | *Devastating centipede.* (23) |

b. Magic animals B151.

| B151. | *Animal determines road to be taken.* (6) |

c. Animals with human traits B240.–B299.7.

B240.	*King of animals.* (29); (49)
B242.	*King of birds.* (50)
B299.7.	*Festival of animals.* (37)

d. Friendly animals B451.+.–B561.+.

B451.+.	*Helpful hummingbird.* (451. *Helpful birds—passeriformes.*) (39)
B455.1.	*Helpful vulture.* (10)
B455.3.	*Helpful eagle.* (49)
B461.1.	*Helpful woodpecker.* (1)
B545.+.	*Tiger rescues man from trap (net).* (B545. *Animal rescues from trap [net].*) (42)
B561.+.	*Animal tells heroine its secret.* (B561. *Animals tell hero their secrets.*) (39)

e. Marriage of person to animal B633.

| B633. | *Human and animal offspring from marriage to animal.* (27) |

f. Fanciful traits of animals B784.1.

| B784.1. | *How animal gets into person's stomach (or body) (various methods).* (22); (23) |

C. TABU

a. Sex tabu C112.–C145.+.

| C112. | *Tabu: sexual intercourse with unearthly beings.* (6) |

156

C114.	*Tabu: incest.* (15); (17)
C140.+.	*Tabu: fishing during menses.* (C140. *Tabu connected with menses.*) (22)
C141.	*Tabu: going forth during menses.* (42); (44)
C142.	*Tabu: sexual intercourse during menses.* (44)
C145.+.	*Tabu: not to touch firestones during menses.* (C145. *Tabu not to touch certain things during menses.*) (5)

b. Speaking tabu C423.3.

| C423.3. | *Tabu: revealing experiences in otherworld.* (6) |

D. MAGIC

a. Transformation D110.+.–D682.3.1.

D110.+.	*Transformation: man to bat.* (D110. *Transformation: man to wild beast [mammal].*) (37)
D110.+.	*Transformation: woman to tapir.* (D110. *Transformation: man to wild beast [mammal].*) (43); (51)
D114.1.1.2.	*Transformation: woman to doe.* (33)
D117.	*Transformation: man to rodent.* (41)
D118.2.	*Transformation: man (woman) to monkey.* (49)
D136.	*Transformation: man to swine.* (29)
D150.	*Transformation: man to bird.* (31)
D195.+.	*Transformation: woman to frog.* (D195. *Transformation: man to frog.*) (2)
D215.	*Transformation: man to tree.* (54)
D281.	*Transformation: man to storm.* (49)
D382.2.	*Transformation: ant to person.* (35)
D415.+.	*Transformation: insect to snake.* (D415. *Transformation: insect to another animal.*) (35)
D429.+.	*Transformation: animal to clay pipe.* (D429. *Transformation: animal to object—misc.*) (40)
D431.2.	*Transformation: tree to person.* (25)
D435.1.1.	*Transformation: statue comes to life.* (25)
D441.+.	*Transformation: wooden disk to animal.* (D441. *Transformation: vegetable form to animal.*) (32)
D451.1.+.	*Transformation: trees to field.* (D451.1. *Transformation: tree to other object.*) (43)
D646.2.	*Transformation to child or pet to be adopted.* (41)

157

D658.2.		*Transformation to husband's (lover's) form to seduce woman.* (45)
D681.		*Gradual transformation.* (37)
D682.3.1.		*Animals in human form retain animal food and habits.* (36)

b. Magic objects D932.–D1402.19.

D932.	*Magic mountain.* (49)
D1002.1.	*Magic urine.* (41)
D1344.+.	*Magic juice gives invulnerability.* (D1344. *Magic object gives invulnerability.*) (17)
D1381.	*Magic object protects from attack.* (9)
D1402.19.	*Magic statue kills.* (9)

c. Magic persons and manifestations D1810.8.3.1.–D2162.

D1810.8.3.1.	*Warning in dream fulfilled.* (20)
D1810.8.3.2.	*Dream warns of danger which will happen in near future.* (20)
D1812.3.3.5.	*Prophetic dream allegorical.* (20)
D1812.5.1.2.	*Bad dream as evil omen.* (20)
D1980.	*Magic invisibility.* (13)
D2060.	*Death or bodily injury by magic.* (49)
D2061.	*Magic murder.* (9)
D2121.5.+.	*Magic journey: woman carried to sky by rainbow.* (D2121.5. *Magic journey: man carried by spirit or devil.*) (4)
D2125.1.	*Magic power to walk on water.* (10)
D2151.0.3.	*Wall of water magically warded off.* (42)
D2157.2.	*Magic quick growth of crops.* (41)
D2157.6.	*Field cultivated and sowed by magic.* (40)
D2161.1.+.	*Magic control of specific diseases.* (D2161.1. *Magic cure for specific diseases.*) (15)
D2162.	*Magic control of disease.* (15)

E. THE DEAD

a. Resuscitation E151.

E151.	*Repeated resuscitation.* (15)

b. Ghosts and other revenants E310.–E752.5.+.

E310.	*Dead lover's friendly return.* (6)
E420.+.	*Revenant as cloud and wind.* (E420. *Appearance of revenant.*) (6)
E481.2.	*Land of dead across water.* (6)
E545.13.	*Man converses with dead.* (6)
E546.	*The dead sing.* (18)
E752.5.+.	*Dogs accompany soul to otherworld.* (E752. *Hell-hounds accompany soul to lower world.*) (6)

F. MARVELS

a. Otherworld journeys F16.–F183.+.

F16.	*Visit to land of moon.* (7); (42)
F92.6.	*Entrance to lower world through cave.* (8)
F101.	*Return from lower world.* (6)
F141.1.	*River as barrier to otherworld.* (6)
F148.	*Wall around otherworld.* (6)
F150.3.	*Challenge at entrance of otherworld.* (6)
F151.1.	*Perilous path to otherworld.* (6)
F151.1.3.	*Perilous forest on way to otherworld.* (6)
F151.1.4.	*Perilous ford on way to otherworld.* (6)
F152.	*Bridge to otherworld.* (6)
F163.	*Buildings in otherworld.* (6)
F164.	*Habitable caves and mounds in otherworld.* (42)
F167.2.	*Dwarfs in otherworld.* (8)
F168.	*Villages in otherworld.* (6)
F183.+.	*Dwarfs eat smoke.* (F183. *Foods in otherworld.*) (8)

b. Marvelous creatures F262.7.+.–F687.

F262.7.+.	*Spirits whistle.* (F262.7. *Fairies whistle.*) (47)
F401.	*Appearance of spirits.* (45)
F401.5.	*Spirits appear horrible.* (44); (46)
F401.9.	*Spirit with feet turned wrong way.* (46)
F402.1.4.+.	*Spirit assumes human form in order to deceive.* (F402.1.4. *Demons assume human forms in order to deceive.*) (45)
F402.1.10.	*Spirit pursues person.* (47)
F402.1.11.	*Spirit causes death.* (47)
F402.1.11.2.	*Evil spirit kills and eats person.* (44)
F402.1.12.	*Spirit fights against person.* (46)
F405.	*Means of combating spirits.* (47)
F406.	*Spirits propitiated.* (50)
F420.6.1.7.+.	*Night spirit surprises and rapes mortal woman.* (F420.6.1.7. *Water spirit surprises and rapes mortal woman.*) (44)
F441.	*Wood spirit.* (46)
F451.1.	*Origin of dwarfs.* (8)
F451.2.3.1.	*Long-bearded dwarfs.* (8)
F451.2.4.+.	*Dwarfs have no hair.* (F451.2.4. *The hair of dwarfs.*) (8)
F451.5.1.	*Helpful dwarfs.* (8)
F451.5.1.7.	*Dwarfs serve mortals.* (16)
F451.5.1.20.	*Dwarfs help in performing task.* (16)
F451.5.11.	*Dwarfs suffer abuses by mortals.* (16)

F451.5.23.		*Dwarfs seek human help in their fights and troubles.* (8)
F451.6.3.4.		*Dwarf dances.* (8)
F470.		*Night spirits.* (44); (47)
F521.1.		*Man covered with hair like animal.* (11)
F529.2.+.		*Dwarfs have no anus.* (F529.2. *People without anuses.*) (8)
F547.1.1.		*Vagina dentata.* (23)
F547.2.		*Hermaphrodite.* (26)
F561.		*People of unusual diet.* (8)
F562.2.		*Residence in tree.* (37)
F565.		*Women warriors or hunters.* (14)
F660.		*Remarkable skill.* (36)
F687.		*Remarkable fragrance (odor) or person.* (41)

c. Extraordinary places and things F771.1.+.–F811.20.

F771.1.+.		*House made of snakes.* (F771.1. *Castle of unusual material.*) (48)
F771.5.1.+.		*Magic mountain guarded by eagle.* (F771.5.1. *Castle guarded by beasts.*) (49)
F807.1.+.		*Red rock.* (F807.1. *Crimson rock.*) (12)
F809.4.		*Bleeding rock.* (10)
F811.7.		*Tree with extraordinary fruit.* (49)
F811.20.		*Bleeding tree.* (1)

d. Extraordinary occurrences F943.1.+.–F1021.+.

F943.1.+.		*Woman sinks into stone.* (F943.1. *Man sinks into stone.*) (12)
F961.1.+.		*Sun stands still.* (F961.1. *Extraordinary behavior of sun.*) (15)
F1021.+.		*Extraordinary flights through air by snake.* (F1021. *Extraordinary flights through air.*) (49)

G. OGRES

a. Kinds of ogres G61.+.–G346.2.

G61.+.		*Lover's flesh eaten unwittingly.* (G61. *Relatives' flesh eaten unwittingly.*) (28)
G77.+.		*Husband eats wife and children.* (G77. *Husband eats wife.*) (11)
G302.9.2.+.		*Demons abduct man.* (G302.9.2. *Demons abduct men and torment them.*) (47)
G346.2.		*Devastating demon.* (46)

b. Falling into ogre's power G441.

G441.		*Ogre carries victim in bag (basket).* (47)

H. TESTS

a. Identity tests; recognition H50.

H50.		*Recognition by bodily marks or physical attributes.* (45)

160

b. Tests of prowess: tasks H976.
H976.   *Task performed by mysterious stranger.* (5)
c. Tests of prowess: quests H1250.1.
H1250.1.   *Test of hero before journey to otherworld.*
                            (6)
d. Other tests H1569.
H1569.   *Tests of character—misc.* (6)

J. THE WISE AND THE FOOLISH

a. Acquisition and possession of wisdom (knowledge) J130.
J130.   *Wisdom (knowledge) acquired from ani-*
                            mals. (39)
b. Wise and unwise conduct J652.—J670.
J652.   *Inattention to warnings.* (42); (45)
J670.   *Forethought in defenses against others.* (14)
c. Fools (and other unwise persons) J1732.—J1919.
J1732.   *Ignorance of certain foods.* (41)
J1919.   *Fatal disregard of anatomy—misc.* (8)

K. DECEPTIONS

a. Deceptive bargains K194.+.
K194.+.   *Bargain: if the sun resumes its course.*
                            (K194. Bargain: if the sun reverses its
                            course.) (15)
b. Thefts and cheats K344.2.+.
K344.2.+.   *Spoiling field with urine.* (K344.2. *Spoiling*
                            rice field with dung.) (40)
c. Escape by deception K500.
K500.   *Escape from death or danger by deception.*
                            (14)
d. Capture by deception K710.—K778.1.
K710.   *Victim enticed into voluntary captivity or*
                            helplessness. (10)
K778.1.   *Amazon overcomes enemies singly.* (14)
e. Fatal deception K834.+.—K951.0.1.+.
K834.+.   *Victims killed while asleep in killer's camp.*
                            (K834. Victim killed while asleep in killer's
                            house.) (11)
K951.0.1.+.   *Deserted wife poisons departing husband.*
                            (K951.0.1. Deserted wife chokes departing
                            husband.) (9)
f. Deception into self-injury K1113.+.
K1113.+.   *Abandonment on tree.* (K1113. *Abandon-*
                            ment on stretching tree.) (10)
g. Seduction or deceptive marriage K1326.—K1326.+.
K1326.   *Seduction by feigned illness.* (17)
K1326.+.   *Attempted seduction by feigned illness.*
                            (K1326. Seduction by feigned illness.) (24)

h. Deception through shams K1822.—K1968.

K1822.	*Animal disguises as human being.* (36)
K1968.	*Sham prowess in hunting (fishing).* (30)

j. False accusation K2100.

K2100.	*False accusation.* (18)

k. Villains and traitors K2212.0.1.+.—K2295.4.+.

K2212.0.1.+.	*Treacherous sister poisons brother.* (K2212.0.1. *Treacherous sister attempts to poison brother.*) (21)
K2213.	*Treacherous wife.* (43)
K2218.	*Treacherous relatives-in-law.* (24)
K2231.	*Treacherous mistress.* (9)
K2247.	*Treacherous lord.* (16)
K2294.	*Treacherous host.* (11)
K2295.4.+.	*Treacherous snake.* (2295.4. *Treacherous lizard.*) (34)

M. ORDAINING THE FUTURE

a. Bargains and promises M205.—M244.

M205.	*Breaking of bargains or promises.* (38); (39)
M244.	*Bargains between men and animals.* (38); (39)

N. CHANCE AND FATE

a. The ways of luck and fate N250.

N250.	*Persistent bad luck.* (30)

b. Unlucky accidents N300.—N350.+.

N300.	*Unlucky accidents.* (41)
N350.+.	*Accidental loss of arrow.* (N350. *Accidental loss of property.*) (7)

c. Accidental encounters N741.—N771.+.

N741.	*Unexpected meeting of husband and wife.* (6)
N771.+.	*Man lost on hunt has adventures.* (N771. *King [prince] lost on hunt has adventures.*) (7); (42)

d. Helpers N810.4.

N810.4.	*Supernatural helper comes from sky.* (10)

Q. REWARDS AND PUNISHMENTS

a. Deeds rewarded Q1.

Q1.	*Hospitality rewarded—opposite punished.* (41)

b. Deeds punished Q211.8.—Q321.

Q211.8.	*Punishment for desire to murder.* (9)
Q211.9.	*Fratricide punished.* (21)
Q253.1.	*Bestiality punished.* (28)

Q266.	*Punishment for breaking promise.* (38); (39)
Q276.	*Stinginess punished.* (19)
Q281.	*Ingratitude punished.* (36)
Q321.	*Laziness punished.* (51)

c. Kinds of punishment Q411.–Q556.

Q411.	*Death as punishment.* (19)
Q411.6.	*Death as punishment for murder.* (11); (21)
Q415.3.	*Punishment: man eaten by worms (snake).* (20)
Q415.3.+.	*Punishment: woman eaten by worms.* (Q415.3. *Punishment: man eaten by worms* [*snake*].) (19); (22)
Q433.	*Punishment: imprisonment.* (29)
Q467.3.+.	*Drowning in swamp.* (Q467.3. *Punishment: drowning in swamp.*) (13)
Q551.3.2.3.	*Punishment: transformation into frog.* (2)
Q552.2.3.	*Earth swallowings as punishment.* (18)
Q552.3.1.	*Famine as punishment.* (15)
Q556.	*Curse as punishment.* (43)

R. CAPTIVES AND FUGITIVES

a. Captivity R39.+.

R39.+.	*Abduction by rainbow.* (R39. *Abduction— misc.*) (4)

b. Rescues R111.6.

R111.6.	*Girl rescued and then abandoned.* (10)

S. UNNATURAL CRUELTY

a. Cruel relatives S62.–S74.1.+.

S62.	*Cruel husband.* (17)
S73.1.	*Fratricide.* (21)
S74.1.+.	*Nephew kills aunt.* (S74.1. *Nephew* [*niece*] *kills uncle.*) (21)

b. Revolting murders or mutilations S111.–S139.2.2.1.+.

S111.	*Murder by poisoning.* (21)
S111.+.	*Attempted murder by poisoning.* (S111. *Murder by poisoning.*) (9)
S112.	*Burning to death.* (37)
S139.+.	*Husband kills wife by urinating in her vagina.* (S139. *Misc. cruel murders.*) (17)
S139.2.2.1.+.	*Heads of spirit impaled upon stake.* (S139.2.2.1. *Heads of slain enemies impaled upon stakes.*) (44)

c. Cruel persecutions S411.

S411.	*Wife banished.* (28)

T. SEX
  a. Marriage T111.5.–T117.5.
      T111.5.   *Marriage of mortal and dwarf.* (8)
      T117.5.   *Marriage with a tree.* (25)
  b. Married life T211.9.–T288.
      T211.9.   *Excessive grief at husband's or wife's death.*
                           (10)
      T288.   *Wife refuses to sleep with detested husband.*
                           (17)
  c. Illicit sexual relations T410.+.–T465.
      T410.+.   *Incest between parallel cousins.* (T410. *In-*
                           cest.) (17)
      T415.   *Brother-sister incest.* (18)
      T417.1.+.   *Mother-in-law seeks to seduce son-in-law.*
                           (T417.1. *Mother-in-law seduces son-in-law.*)
                           (24)
      T461.3.   *Tree as wife.* (25)
      T462.   *Lesbian love.* (26)
      T465.   *Bestiality.* (27); (28); (35)
  d. Conception and birth T523.+.–T554.7.+.
      T523.+.   *Conception from water.* (T523. *Conception*
                           from bathing.) (10)
      T539.6.   *Conception from artificial phallus.* (10)
      T554.7.+.   *Woman gives birth to snakes.* (T554.7.
                           Woman gives birth to a snake.) (35)

V. RELIGION

  a. Religious beliefs V311.
      V311.   *Belief in the life to come.* (1)

W. TRAITS OF CHARACTER

  a. Unfavorable traits of character W111.3.–W195.
      W111.3.   *The lazy wife.* (51)
      W152.   *Stinginess.* (19)
      W154.   *Ingratitude.* (36)
      W154.2.1.   *Rescued animal threatens rescuer.* (34)
      W181.   *Jealousy.* (6)
      W195.   *Envy.* (36)

Z. MISC. GROUPS OF MOTIFS

  a. Heroes Z235.
      Z235.   *Hero with extraordinary animal com-*
                           panions. (41)

Alphabetical Motif Index

ABANDONED.–Girl rescued and then abandoned R111.6. (10)

ABANDONMENT on tree K1113.+. (10)

ABDUCT.–Demons abduct man G302.9.2.+. (47)

ABDUCTION by rainbow R39.+. (4)

ABSENT.–Why certain animals are absent from countries A2434.2. (40)

ABUSES.–Dwarfs suffer abuses . . . F451.5.11. (16)

ACCIDENTAL loss of arrow N350.+. (7)

ACCIDENTS.–Unlucky accidents N300. (41)

ACCOMPANY.–Dogs accompany soul . . . E752.5.+. (6)

ACCUSATION.–False accusation K2100. (18)

ACQUIRED.–Animal characteristics acquired during flood A2291.+. (3); wisdom (knowledge) acquired from animals J130. (39)

ACQUISITION of agriculture A1441. (42); of manioc A1423.4. (7); (42)

ADOPTED.–Transformation to child or pet to be adopted D646.2. (41)

ADVENTURES.–Man lost on hunt has adventures N771.+. (7); (42)

AGRICULTURE.–Acquisition of agriculture A1441. (42)

AIR.–Extraordinary flights through air . . . F1021.+. (49)

ALLEGORICAL.–Prophetic dream allegorical D1812.3.3.5. (20)

AMAZON overcomes enemies singly K778.1. (14)

ANATOMY.–Fatal disregard of anatomy–misc. J1919. (8)

ANCIENT.–Present habitat of trees result of ancient quarrel A2282.+. (54)

ANIMAL characteristics acquired during flood A2291.+. (3); determines road to be taken B151. (6); disguises as human being K1822. (36); tells heroine its secret B561.+. (39).–Hero with extraordinary animal companions Z235. (41); how animal gets into person's stomach . . . B784. 1. (22); (23); human and animal offspring . . . B633. (27); man covered with hair like animal F521.1. (11); parts of human or animal body transformed . . . A2611.0.5. (41); rescued animal threatens rescuer W154.2.1. (34); transformation: animal to clay pipe D429.+. (40); transformation: wooden disk to animal D441.+. (32)

ANIMALS in human form retain animal food and habits D682.3.1. (36).–Bargains between men and animals M244. (38); (39); festival of animals B299.7. (37); friendships between animals A2493. (32); king of animals B240. (29); (49); why certain animals are absent from countries A2434.2. (40); why there is enmity between certain animals and man A2585. (38); wisdom (knowledge) acquired from animals J130. (39)

ANT.–Transformation: ant to person D382.2. (35)

ANUS.–Dwarfs have no anus F529.2.+. (8)

APPEAR.–Spirits appear horrible F401.5. (44); (46)

APPEARANCE of spirits F401. (45)

ARROW.–Accidental loss of arrow N350.+. (7)

ARTIFICIAL.–Conception from artificial phallus T539.6. (10)
ARTS.–Culture hero teaches arts and crafts A541. (41)
ASLEEP.–Victims killed while asleep in killer's camp K834.+. (11)
ATTACK.–Magic object protects from attack D1381. (9)
ATTEMPTED murder by poisoning S111.+. (9); seduction by feigned
    illness K1326.+. (24)
ATTRIBUTES.–Recognition by . . . physical attributes H50. (45)
AUNT.–Nephew kills aunt S74.1.+. (21)
BAD dream as evil omen D1812.5.1.2. (20)
BAD LUCK.–Persistent bad luck N250. (30)
BANANA.–Origin of banana A2687.5. (7); (41)
BANISHED.–Wife banished S411. (28)
BARGAIN: if the sun resumes its course K194.+. (15)
BARGAINS between men and animals M244. (38); (39).–Breaking of
    bargains or promises M205. (38); (39)
BARRIER.–River as barrier . . . F141.1. (6)
BASKET.–Ogre carries victim in basket G441. (47)
BAT.–Transformation: man to bat D110.+. (37)
BEING.–Animal disguises as human being K1822. (36); tabu: sexual
    intercourse with unearthly beings C112. (6)
BELIEF in the life to come V311. (1)
BESTIALITY. T465. (27); (28); (35); punished Q253.1. (28)
BIRD.–Transformation: man to bird D150. (31)
BIRDS.–Creation of birds A1900. (31); cries of birds A2426.2. (31);
    king of birds B242. (50)
BIRTH.–Woman gives birth to snakes T554.7.+. (35)
BLEEDING rock F809.4. (10); tree F811.20. (1)
BOAR.–Origin of wild boar A1871.1. (52)
BODILY.–Death or bodily injury by magic D2060. (49); recognition
    by bodily marks . . . H50. (45)
BODY.–How animal gets into person's stomach (or body) . . . B784.1.
    (22); (23); parts of human or animal body transformed . . . A2611.0.5.
    (41)
BREAKING of bargains or promises M205. (38); (39).–Flood as punish-
    ment for breaking tabu A1018.1. (15),–Punishment for breaking
    promise Q266. (38); (39)
BREWING.–Introduction of brewing A1426.2.1. (1)
BRIDGE to other world F152. (6)
BROTHER.–Sun and his brother rise and set alternately A736.3.3. (2);
    treacherous sister poisons brother K2212.0.1.+. (21)
BROTHERS.–Sun and moon as brothers A736.3. (2); (42); why brothers
    and sisters do not marry A1552.1. (1)
BROTHER-SISTER incest T415. (18); marriage . . . A1552.3. (1)
BUILDINGS in otherworld F163. (6)
BURNING to death S112. (37)
CALAMITY.–New race . . . after tribal calamity A1006.1.+. (15)
CAMP.–Victims killed while asleep in killer's camp K834.+. (11)

CANNIBAL.—Sun as cannibal A711.2. (7); (42)

CAPTIVITY.—Victim enticed into voluntary captivity . . . K710. (10)

CARRY. Magic journey: woman carried . . . D2121.5.+. (4); Ogre carries victim in basket G441. (47)

CAUSED.—Disease caused by evil spirit A1337.0.2.+. (15)

CAUSES.—Spirit causes death F402.1.11. (47)

CAVE.—Entrance to lower world through cave F92.6. (8)

CAVES.—Habitable caves . . . F164. (42)

CENTIPEDE.—Devastating centipede B16.6.5. (23)

CHALLENGE at entrance of otherworld F150.3. (6)

CHARACTER.—Tests of character—misc. H1569. (6)

CHARACTERISTICS.—Animal characteristics acquired during flood A2291.+. (3)

CHILD.—Transformation to child or pet . . . D646.2. (41)

CHILDREN.—Brother-sister marriage of children of first parents A1552.3. (1); husband eats wife and children G77.+. (11); stars as children . . . A764.1. (42)

CLAY.—Origin of clay A998. (40); transformation: animal to clay pipe D429.+. (40)

CLOUD.—Revenant as cloud and wind E420.+. (6)

COMBATING spirits, Means of F405. (47)

COMPANIONS.—Hero with extraordinary animal companions Z235. (41)

CONCEPTION from artificial phallus T539.6. (10); from water T523.+. (10)

CONTROL.—Magic control of disease D2162. (15); magic control of specific diseases D2161.1.+. (15)

CONVERSES.—Man converses with dead E545.13. (6)

COTTON.—Origin of cotton plant A2684.3. (7)

COUNTRIES.—Why certain animals are absent from countries A2434.2. (40)

COURSE.—Bargain: if the sun resumes its course K194.+. (15)

COUSINS.—Incest between parallel cousins T410.+. (17)

CRAFTS.—Culture hero teaches arts and crafts A541. (41)

CREATION of birds A1900. (31); of man . . . A1252. (1); of the moon A740. (2)

CREATOR.—Creator's wife A32.3. (1)

CRIES of birds A2426.2. (31)

CROPS.—Magic quick growth of crops D2157.2. (41)

CRUEL husband S62. (17)

CULTIVATED.—Field cultivated and sowed by magic D2157.6. (40)

CULTURE HERO establishes customs A545. (1); performs remarkable feats . . . A526.7. (13); teaches . . . A541. (41).—Culture hero's (demi-god's) departure A560. (41)

CURSE as punishment Q556. (43)

CUSTOMS.—Culture hero establishes customs A545. (1)

DANCE.—Dwarf dances F451.6.3.4. (8)

DANGER.–Dream warns of danger . . . D1810.8.3.2. (20); escape from death or danger by deception K500. (14)

DAY.–Origin of night and day A1170. (2)

DEAD lover's friendly return E310. (6).–Land of dead across water E481.2. (6); man converses with dead E545.13. (6); the dead sing E546. (18)

DEATH as punishment Q411. (19); as punishment for murder Q411.6. (11); (21); or bodily injury by magic D2060. (49).–Burning to death S112. (37); escape from death or danger by deception K500. (14); excessive grief at husband's or wife's death T211.9. (10); spirit causes death F402.1.11. (47)

DECEIVE.–Moon deceives sun A753.3.1. (42); spirit assumes human form in order to deceive F402.1.4.+. (45)

DECEPTION.–Escape from death or danger by deception K500. (14)

DEFENSES.–Forethought in defenses . . . J670. (14)

DELUGE.–Bringing deluge to end A1028. (15); escape from deluge on mountain A1022. (3); sun does not shine during deluge A1010.1. (15)

DEMIGOD.–Culture hero's (demigod's) departure A560. (41)

DEMON.–Devastating demon G346.2. (46)

DEMONS abduct man G302.9.2.+. (47)

DEPARTING.–Deserted wife poisons departing husband K951.0.1.+. (9)

DEPARTURE.–Culture hero's (demigod's) departure A560. (41)

DESERTED wife poisons . . . K951.0.1.+. (9)

DESIRE.–Punishment for desire to murder Q211.8. (9)

DETERMINES.–Animal determines road to be taken B151. (6)

DETESTED.–Wife refuses to sleep with detested husband T288. (17)

DEVASTATING centipede B16.6.5. (23); demon G346.2. (46)

DIET.–People of unusual diet F561. (8)

DISEASE caused by evil spirit A1337.0.2.+. (15).–Magic control of disease D2162. (15); origin of disease A1337. (15)

DISEASES.–Magic control of specific diseases D2161.1.+. (15)

DISGUISE.–Animal disguises as human being K1822. (36)

DISK.–Transformation: wooden disk to animal D441.+. (32)

DISPOSITION.–Mental powers and disposition of sun A738.2. (42)

DISREGARD.–Fatal disregard of anatomy—misc. J1919. (8)

DISTRIBUTION of tribes A1620. (13)

DIVER.–Earth diver A812. (3)

DOE.–Transformation: woman to doe D114.1.1.2. (33)

DOGS accompany soul . . . E752.5.+. (6)

DREAM warns of danger . . . D1810.8.3.2. (20).–Bad dream as evil omen D1812.5.1.2. (20); prophetic dream allegorical D1812.3.3.5. (20); warning in dream fulfilled D1810.8.3.1. (20)

DROWNING in swamp Q467.3.+. (13)

DWARF dances F451.6.3.4. (8).–Marriage of mortal and dwarf T111.5. (8)

DWARFS eat smoke F183.+. (8); have no anus F529.2.+. (8); have no hair F451.2.4.+. (8); help in performing task F451.5.1.20. (16); in otherworld F167.2. (8); seek human help . . . F451.5.23. (8); serve mortals F451.5.1.7. (16); suffer abuses . . . F451.5.11. (16).—Helpful dwarfs F451.5.1. (8), long-bearded dwarfs F451.2.3.1. (8); origin of dwarfs F451.1. (8)

EAGLE.—Helpful eagle B455.3. (49); magic mountain guarded by eagle F771.5.1.+. (49)

EARTH diver A812. (3); swallowings . . . Q552.2.3. (18)

EAT.—Dwarfs eat smoke. F183.+. (8); evil spirit kills and eats person F402.1.11.2. (44); husband eats wife and children G77.+. (11)

EATEN.—Lover's flesh eaten unwittingly G61.+. (28); punishment: man eaten . . . Q415.3. (20); punishment: woman eaten . . . Q415.3.+. (19); (22)

END.—Bringing deluge to end A1028. (15)

ENDOWED.—Moon endowed . . . A753.3.4. (42)

ENEMIES.—Amazon overcomes enemies singly K778.1. (14)

ENMITY.—Why there is enmity between certain animals and man A2585. (38); why there is enmity between snakes and man A2585.+. (53); why there is enmity between tigers and man A2585.+. (46)

ENTICED.—Victim enticed . . . K710. (10)

ENTRANCE to lower world through cave F92.6. (8).—Challenge at entrance of otherworld F150.3. (6)

ENVY. W195. (36)

ESCAPE from death or danger by deception K500. (14); from deluge on mountain A1022. (3)

ESTABLISH.—Culture hero establishes customs A545. (1)

EVIL spirit kills and eats person F402.1.11.2. (44).—Bad dream as evil omen D1812.5.1.2. (20); disease caused by evil spirit A1337.0.2.+. (15)

EXCESSIVE grief . . . T211.9. (10)

EXPERIENCES.—Tabu: revealing experiences . . . C423.3. (6)

EXTRAORDINARY flights through air . . . F1021.+. (49).—Hero with extraordinary animal companions Z235. (41); tree with extraordinary fruit F811.7. (49)

FALSE accusation K2100. (18)

FAMILY of the moon A745. (2); (42)

FAMINE as punishment Q552.3.1. (15)

FATAL disregard of anatomy—misc. J1919. (8)

FEATS.—Culture hero performs remarkable feats . . . A526.7. (13)

FEET.—Spirit with feet turned wrong way F401.9. (46)

FEIGNED.—Attempted seduction by feigned illness K1326.+. (24) seduction by feigned illness K1326. (17)

FESTIVAL of animals B299.7. (37)

FIELD cultivated and sowed by magic D2157.6. (40).—Spoiling field with urine K344.2.+. (40); transformation: trees to field D451.1.+. (43)

FIGHT.—Spirit fights against person F402.1.12. (46)

FIGHTS.—Dwarfs seek human help in their fights . . . F451.5.23. (8)

FIRE.—Origin of fire . . . A1414.4. (5); sun thrown on fire A1068.+. (2)

FIRESTONES.—Tabu: not to touch firestones . . . C145.+. (5)

FIRST.—Brother-sister marriage of children of first parents A1552.3. (1); incestuous first parents A1273.1. (1); or origin of first parents A1271. (1)

FISHING.—Sham prowess in hunting (fishing) K1968. (30); tabu: fishing during menses C140.+. (22)

FLESH.—Lover's flesh eaten unwittingly G61.+. (28)

FLIGHTS.—Extraordinary flights through air . . . F1021.+. (49)

FLINT.—Origin of flint . . . A1414.5. (5)

FLOOD.—A1009.+. (3); as punishment for breaking tabu A1018.1. (15); as punishment for incest A1018.2. (15).—Animal characteristics acquired during flood A2291.+. (3)

FOOD.—Animals in human form retain animal food and habits D682.3.1. (36)

FOODS.—Ignorance of certain foods J1732. (41)

FORD.—Perilous ford . . . F151.1.4. (6)

FOREST.—Perilous forest . . . F151.1.3. (6)

FORETHOUGHT in defenses against others J670. (14)

FORM.—Animals in human form retain animal food and habits D682.3.1. (36); spirit assumes human form . . . F402.1.4.+. (45); transformation to husband's (lover's) form to seduce woman D658.2. (45)

FORTH.—Tabu: going forth during menses C141. (42); (44)

FRAGRANCE.—Remarkable fragrance . . . F687. (41)

FRATRICIDE. S73.1. (21); punished Q211.9. (21)

FRIENDLY.—Dead lover's friendly return E310. (6)

FRIENDSHIPS between animals A2493. (32)

FROG.—Punishment: transformation into frog Q551.3.2.3. (2); transformation: woman to frog D195.+. (2)

FRUIT.—Tree with extraordinary fruit F811.7. (49)

FULFILLED.—Warning in dream fulfilled D1810.8.3.1. (20)

FUTURE.—Dream warns of danger which will happen in near future D1810.8.3.2. (20)

GIFT.—Origin of fire—gift from god A1414.4. (5)

GIRL rescued . . . R111.6. (10)

GOD makes wooden images . . . A141.1.+. (1).—Origin of fire—gift from god A1414.4. (5)

GRADUAL transformation D681. (37)

GRIEF.—Excessive grief . . . T211.9. (10)

GROWTH.—Magic quick growth of crops D2157.2. (41)

GUARDED.—Magic mountain guarded . . . F771.5.1.+. (49)

HABITABLE caves . . . F164. (42)

HABITAT.—Present habitat of trees . . . A2282.+. (54)

HABITS.–Animals in human form retain animal food and habits D682.3.1. (36)

HAIR.–Dwarfs have no hair F451.2.4.+. (8); man covered with hair . . . F521.1. (11)

HEAD of spirit impaled . . . S139.2.2.1.+. (44)

HELP.–Dwarfs help in performing task F451.5.1.20. (16); dwarfs seek human help . . . F451.5.23. (8)

HELPER.–Supernatural helper . . . N810.4. (10)

HELPFUL dwarfs F451.5.1. (8); eagle B455.3. (49); hummingbird B451.+. (39); vulture B455.1. (10); woodpecker B461.1. (1)

HELPLESSNESS.–Victim enticed into . . . helplessness K710. (10)

HERMAPHRODITE. F547.2. (26)

HERO with extraordinary animal companions Z235. (41).–Test of hero before journey . . . H1250.1. (6)

HEROINE.–Animal tells heroine its secret B561.+. (39)

HORRIBLE.–Spirits appear horrible F401.5. (44); (46)

HOSPITALITY rewarded–opposite punished Q1. (41)

HOST.–Treacherous host K2294. (11)

HOUSE made of snakes F771.1.+. (48).–Moon has house A753.2. (42); (48)

HUMAN and animal offspring . . . B633. (27).–Animals in human form . . . D682.3.1. (36); dwarfs seek human help . . . F451.5.23. (8); parts of human or animal body transformed . . . A2611.0.5. (41); spirit assumes human form . . . F402.1.4.+. (45)

HUMAN BEING.–Animal disguises as human being K1822. (36)

HUMMINGBIRD.–Helpful hummingbird B451.+. (39)

HUNT.–Man lost on hunt . . . N771.+. (7); (42)

HUNTERS.–Women warriors or hunters F565. (14)

HUNTING.–Sham prowess in hunting (fishing) K1968. (30)

HUSBAND eats wife and children G77.+. (11); kills wife by urinating . . . S139.+. (17).–Cruel husband S62. (17); deserted wife poisons departing husband K951.0.1.+. (9); excessive grief at husband's . . . death T211.9. (10); transformation to husband's (lover's) form to seduce woman D658.2. (45); unexpected meeting of husband and wife N741. (6); wife refuses to sleep with detested husband T288. (17)

IGNORANCE of certain foods J1732. (41)

ILLNESS.–Attempted seduction by feigned illness K1326.+. (24); seduction by feigned illness K1326. (17)

IMAGE.–Mankind from vivified wooden image A1252.1. (1)

IMAGES.–God makes wooden images . . . A141.1.+. (1)

IMPALED.–Head of spirit impaled . . . S139.2.2.1.+. (44)

IMPRISONMENT.–Punishment: imprisonment Q433. (29)

INATTENTION to warnings J652. (42); (45)

INCEST between parallel cousins T410.+. (17).–Brother-sister incest T415. (18); flood as punishment for incest A1018.2. (15); tabu: incest C114. (15); (17)

INCESTUOUS first parents A1273.1. (1)

INGRATITUDE. W154. (36); punished Q281. (36)

INJURY.—Death or bodily injury by magic D2060. (49)

INSECT.—Transformation: insect to snake D415. +. (35)

INTERCOURSE.—Tabu: sexual intercourse during menses C142. (44); tabu: sexual intercourse with unearthly beings C112. (6)

INTRODUCTION of brewing A1426.2.1. (1)

INVISIBILITY.—Magic invisibility D1980. (13)

INVULNERABILITY.—Magic juice gives invulnerability D1344. +. (17)

JEALOUSY. W181. (6)

JOURNEY.—Magic journey: woman carried . . . D2121.5. +. (4); test of hero before journey . . . H1250.1. (6)

JUICE.—Magic juice . . . D1344. +. (17)

KILL.—Evil spirit kills . . . F402.1.11.2. (44); husband kills wife by urinating . . . S139. +. (17); magic statue kills D1402.19. (9); nephew kills aunt S74.1. +. (21)

KILLED.—Victims killed while asleep in killer's camp K834. +. (11)

KILLER.—Victims killed while asleep in killer's camp K834. +. (11)

KING of animals B240. (29); (49); of birds B242. (50)

KNOWLEDGE.—Wisdom (knowledge) acquired from animals J130. (39)

LAND of dead across water E481.2. (6).—Visit to land of moon F16. (7); (42)

LAZINESS punished Q321. (51)

LAZY wife W111.3. (51)

LESBIAN love T462. (26)

LIFE.—Belief in the life to come V311. (1); transformation: statue comes to life D435.1.1. (25)

LONG-BEARDED dwarfs F451.2.3.1. (8)

LORD of particular mountain A418. +. (49).—Treacherous lord K2247. (16)

LOSS.—Accidental loss of arrow N350. +. (7)

LOST.—Man lost on hunt . . . N771. +. (7); (42)

LOVE.—Lesbian love T462. (26)

LOVER.—Dead lover's friendly return E310. (6); lover's flesh eaten unwittingly G61. +. (28); transformation to husband's (lover's) form . . . D658.2. (45)

LOWER WORLD.—Entrance to lower world through cave F92.6. (8); return from lower world F101. (6)

LUCK.—Persistent bad luck N250. (30)

MAGIC control of disease D2162. (15); of specific diseases D2161.1. +. (15); invisibility D1980. (13); journey: woman carried . . . D2121.5. +. (4); juice . . . D1344. +. (17); mountain D932. (49); mountain guarded . . . F771.5.1. +. (49); murder D2061. (9); object protects . . . D1381. (9); power to walk on water D2125.1. (10); quick growth . . . D2157.2. (41); statue kills D1402.19. (9); urine D1002.1. (41).—Death or bodily injury by magic D2060. (49); field cultivated and sowed by magic D2157.6. (40)

MAGICALLY.—Wall of water magically warded off D2151.0.3. (42)

MAIZE.—Origin of maize A2685.1.1. (41)

MAN converses with dead E545.13. (6); covered with hair . . . F521.1. (11); lost on hunt . . . N771.+. (7); (42).—Creation of man . . . A1252. (1); demons abduct man G302.9.2.+. (47); origin of white man A1614.9. (10); origin of white man's weapons A1459.1.+. (10); punishment: man eaten . . . Q415.3. (20); tiger rescues man from trap (net) B545.+. (42); transformation: man to bat D110.+. (37); transformation: man to bird D150. (31); transformation: man (woman) to monkey D118.2. (49); transformation: man to rodent D117. (41); transformation: man to storm D281. (49); transformation: man to swine D136. (29); transformation: man to tree D215. (54); why there is enmity between certain animals and man A2585. (38); why there is enmity between snakes and man A2585.+. (53); why there is enmity between tigers and man A2585.+. (46)

MANIOC.—Acquisition of manioc A1423.4. (7); (42)

MANKIND from vivified wooden image A1252.1. (1)

MARKS.—Recognition by bodily marks . . . H50. (45)

MARRIAGE of mortal and dwarf T111.5. (8); with a tree T117.5. (25).—Brother-sister marriage . . . A1552.3. (1); human and animal offspring from marriage to animal B633. (27)

MARRY.—Why brothers and sisters do not marry A1552.1. (1)

MEETING.—Unexpected meeting of husband and wife N741. (6)

MEN.—Bargains between men and animals M244. (38); (39)

MENSES.—Tabu: fishing during menses C140.+. (22); tabu: going forth during menses C141. (42); (44); tabu: not to touch firestones during menses C145.+. (5); tabu: sexual intercourse during menses C142. (44)

MENTAL.—Mental powers . . . A738.2. (42)

MILKY WAY.—Origin of the Milky Way A778. (2)

MISDOING.—Moon's phases as punishment for moon's misdoing A755.6. (2)

MISTRESS.—Treacherous mistress K2231. (9)

MONKEY.—Transformation: man (woman) to monkey D118.2. (49)

MOON deceives sun A753.3.1. (42); endowed with wisdom and passion A753.3.4. (42); has house A753.2. (42); (48).—Creation of the moon A740. (2). family of the moon A745. (2); (42); . . . moon's misdoing A755.6. (2); moon's phases . . . A755.6. (2); moon's son . . . A764.1.+. (2); originally two suns but no moon A711.3.+. (2); stars as children of the moon A764.1. (42); sun and moon as brothers A736.3. (2); (42); visit to land of moon F16. (7); (42); why the moon is pale A759.3. (2)

MORTAL.—Marriage of mortal and dwarf T111.5. (8); night spirit surprises and rapes mortal woman F420.6.1.7.+. (44)

MORTALS.—Dwarfs serve mortals F451.5.1.7. (16); dwarfs suffer abuses by mortals F451.5.11. (16)

MOTHER-IN-LAW seeks to seduce son-in-law T417.1.+. (24)

MOUNDS.—Habitable caves and mounds . . . F164. (42)

MOUNTAIN.—Escape from deluge on mountain A1022. (3); lord of particular mountain A418. +. (49); magic mountain D932. (49); magic mountain guarded . . . F771.5.1.+. (49)

MURDER by poisoning S111. (21).—Attempted murder by poisoning S111.+. (9); death as punishment for murder Q411.6. (11); (21); magic murder D2061. (9); punishment for desire to murder Q211.8. (9)

MYSTERIOUS.—Task performed by mysterious stranger H976. (5).

NEPHEW kills aunt S74.1.+. (21)

NET.—Tiger rescues man from trap (net) B545.+. (42)

NIGHT.—Origin of night and day A1170. (2)

NIGHT SPIRIT surprises and rapes mortal woman F420.6.1.7.+. (44)

NIGHT SPIRITS F470. (44); (47)

ODOR.—Remarkable fragrance (odor) of person F687. (41)

OFFSPRING.—Human and animal offspring . . . B633. (27)

OGRE carries victim in basket G441. (47)

OMEN.—Bad dream as evil omen D1812.5.1.2. (20)

OPPOSITE.—Hospitality rewarded—opposite punished Q1. (41)

ORIGIN of banana A2687.5. (7); (41); of clay A998. (40); of cotton plant A2684.3. (7); of disease A1337. (15); of dwarfs F451.1. (8); of fire . . . A1414.4. (5); of first parents A1271. (1); of flint . . . A1414.5. (5); of maize A2685.1.1. (41); of Milky Way A778. (2); of night and day A1170. (2); of tapir A1889.1.+. (51); of white man A1614.9. (10); of white man's weapons A1459.1.+. (10); of wild boar A1871.1. (52); of yams A2686.4.3. (7)

ORIGINALLY two suns . . . A711.3.+. (2)

OTHERWORLD.—Bridge to otherworld F152. (6); buildings in otherworld F163. (6); challenge at entrance of otherworld F150.3. (6); dogs accompany soul to otherworld E752.5.+. (6); dwarfs in otherworld F167.2. (8); habitable caves and mounds in otherworld F164. (42); perilous ford on way to otherworld F151.1.4. (6); perilous forest on way to otherworld F151.1.3. (6); perilous path to otherworld F151.1. (6); river as barrier to otherworld F141.1. (6); tabu: revealing experiences in otherworld C423.3. (6); test of hero before journey to otherworld H1250.1. (6); villages in otherworld F168. (6); wall around otherworld F148. (6)

OVERCOME.—Amazon overcomes enemies singly K778.1. (14)

PAIR.—New race from single pair (or several) after tribal calamity A1006.1.+. (15)

PALE.—Why the moon is pale A759.3. (2)

PARALLEL COUSINS.—Incest between parallel cousins T410.+. (17)

PARENTS.—Brother-sister marriage of children of first parents A1552.3. (1); incestuous first parents A1273.1. (1); origin of first parents A1271. (1)

PARTS of human or animal body transformed . . . A2611.0.5. (41)

PASSION.—Moon endowed with wisdom and passion A753.3.4. (42)

PATH.—Perilous path to otherworld F151.1. (6)

PEOPLE of unusual diet F561. (8)

PERFORM.–Culture hero performs remarkable feats . . . A526.7. (13)

PERFORMED.–Task performed by mysterious stranger H976. (5)

PERFORMING.–Dwarfs help in performing task F451.5.1.20. (16)

PERILOUS ford . . . F151.1.4. (6); forest . . . F151.1.3. (6); path to otherworld F151.1. (6)

PERSISTENT bad luck N250. (30)

PERSON.–Evil spirit kills and eats person F402.1.11.2. (44); how animal gets into person's stomach . . . B784.1. (22); (23); remarkable fragrance (odor) of person F687. (41); spirit fights against person F402.1.12. (46); spirit pursues person F402.1.10. (47); transformation: ant to person D382.2. (35); transformation: tree to person D431.2. (25)

PET.–Transformation to child or pet to be adopted D646.2. (41)

PHALLUS.–Conception from artificial phallus T539.6. (10)

PHASES.–Moon's phases . . . A755.6. (2)

PHYSICAL.–Recognition by . . . physical attributes H50. (45)

PIPE.–Transformation: animal to clay pipe D429.+. (40)

PLANT.–Origin of cotton plant A2684.3. (7)

PLANTS.–Parts of human or animal body transformed into plants A2611.0.5. (41)

POISON.–Deserted wife poisons . . . K951.0.1.+. (9); treacherous sister poisons brother K2212.0.1.+. (21)

POISONING.–Attempted murder by poisoning S111.+. (9); murder by poisoning S111. (21)

POWER.–Magic power to walk . . . D2125.1. (10)

POWERS.–Mental powers . . . A738.2. (42)

PRESENT habitat of trees . . . A2282.+. (54)

PROMISE.–Punishment for breaking promise Q266. (38); (39)

PROMISES.–Breaking of bargains or promises M205. (38); (39)

PROPHETIC dream allegorical D1812.3.3.5. (20)

PROPITIATED.–Spirits propitiated F406. (50)

PROTECT.–Magic object protects from attack D1381. (9)

PROWESS.–Sham prowess in hunting (fishing) K1968. (30)

PUNISHED.–Bestiality punished Q253.1. (28); fratricide punished Q211.9. (21); hospitality rewarded–opposite punished Q1. (41); ingratitude punished Q281. (36); laziness punished Q321. (51); stinginess punished Q276. (19)

PUNISHMENT for breaking promise Q266. (38); (39); for desire to murder Q211.8. (9); imprisonment Q433. (29); man eaten by worms (snake) Q415.3. (20); transformation into frog Q551.3.2.3. (2); woman eaten . . . Q415.3.+. (19); (22).–Curse as punishment Q556. (43); death as punishment Q411. (19); death as punishment for murder Q441.6. (11); (21); earth swallowings as punishment Q552.2.3. (18); famine as punishment Q552.3.1. (15); flood as punishment for breaking tabu A1018.1. (15); flood as punishment for incest A1018.2. (15); moon's phases as punishment . . . A755.6. (2)

PURSUE.–Spirit pursues person F402.1.10. (47)

QUARREL.–Present habitat of trees result of ancient quarrel A2282.+. (54)

QUICK.–Magic quick growth . . . D2157.2. (41)

RACE.–New race from single pair (or several) after tribal calamity A1006.1.+. (15)

RAINBOW.–Abduction by rainbow R39.+. (4); magic journey: woman carried to sky by rainbow D2121.5.+. (4)

RAPE.–Night spirit surprises and rapes mortal woman F420.6.1.7.+. (44)

RECOGNITION by bodily marks . . . H50. (45)

RED rock F807.1.+. (12)

REFUSE.–Wife refuses to sleep with detested husband T288. (17)

RELATIVES-IN-LAW.–Treacherous relatives-in-law K2218. (24)

REMARKABLE fragrance (odor) of person F687. (41); skill F660. (36).–Culture hero performs remarkable feats . . . A526.7. (13)

REPEATED resuscitation E151. (15)

RESCUE.–Tiger rescues man from trap (net) B545.+. (42)

RESCUED animal threatens rescuer W154.2.1. (34).–Girl rescued . . . R111.6. (10)

RESCUER.–Rescued animal threatens rescuer W154.2.1. (34)

RESIDENCE in tree F562.2. (37)

RESULT.–Present habitat of trees result of ancient quarrel A2282.+. (54)

RESUME.–Bargain: if the sun resumes its course K194.+. (15)

RESUSCITATION.–Repeated resuscitation E151. (15)

RETURN from lower world F101. (6).–Dead lover's friendly return E310. (6)

REVEALING.–Tabu: revealing experiences . . . C423.3. (6)

REVENANT as cloud and wind E420.+. (6)

REWARDED.–Hospitality rewarded–opposite punished Q1. (41)

RISE.–Sun and his brother rise and set alternately A736.3.3. (2)

RIVER as barrier . . . F141.1 (6)

ROAD.–Animal determines road to be taken B151. (6)

ROCK.–Bleeding rock F809.4. (10); red rock F807.1.+. (12)

RODENT.–Transformation: man to rodent D117. (41)

SECRET.–Animal tells heroine its secret B561.+. (39)

SEDUCE.–Mother-in-law seeks to seduce son-in-law T417.1.+. (24); transformation . . . to seduce woman D658.2. (45)

SEDUCTION by feigned illness K1326. (17).–Attempted seduction by feigned illness K1326.+. (24)

SEEK.–Dwarfs seek human help . . . F451.5.23. (8); mother-in-law seeks to seduce . . . T417.1.+. (24)

SERVE.–Dwarfs serve mortals F451.5.1.7. (16)

SET.–Sun and his brother rise and set alternately A736.3.3. (2)

SEXUAL.–Tabu: sexual intercourse during menses C142. (44); tabu: sexual intercourse with unearthly beings C112. (6)

SHAM prowess in hunting (fishing) K1968. (30)

SHINE.–Sun does not shine during deluge A1010.1. (15)

SING.–The dead sing E546. (18)

SINGLY.–Amazon overcomes enemies singly K778.1. (14)

SINK.–Woman sinks into stone F943.1.+. (12)

SISTER.–Brother-sister incest T415. (18); brother-sister marriage . . . A1552.3. (1); treacherous sister poisons brother K2212.0.1.+. (21)

SISTERS.–Why brothers and sisters do not marry A1552.1. (1)

SKILL.–Culture hero performs . . . feats of . . . skill A526.7. (13); remarkable skill F660. (36)

SKY.–Magic journey: woman carried to sky . . . D2121.5.+. (4); supernatural helper comes from sky N810.4. (10)

SLEEP.–Wife refuses to sleep with detested husband T288. (17)

SMOKE.–Dwarfs eat smoke F183.+. (8)

SNAKE.–Extraordinary flights through air by snake F1021.+. (49); punishment: man eaten by worms (snake) Q415.3. (20); transformation: insect to snake D415.+. (35); treacherous snake K2295.4.+. (34)

SNAKES.–House made of snakes F771.1.+. (48); why snakes are venomous A2532.1. (53); why there is enmity between snakes and man A2585.+. (53); woman gives birth to snakes T554.7.+. (35)

SON.–Moon's son . . . A764.1.+. (2)

SON-IN-LAW.–Mother-in-law seeks to seduce son-in-law T417.1.+. (24)

SOUL.–Dogs accompany soul . . . E752.5.+. (6)

SOWED.–Field cultivated and sowed by magic D2157.6. (40)

SPECIFIC.–Magic control of specific diseases D2161.1.+. (15)

SPIRIT assumes human form . . . F402.1.4.+. (45); causes death F402.1.11. (47); fights against person F402.1.12. (46); pursues person F402.1.10. (47); with feet turned wrong way F401.9. (46).–Disease caused by evil spirit A1337.0.2.+. (15); evil spirit kills and eats person F402.1.11.2. (44); head of spirit impaled . . . S139.2.2.1.+. (44); night spirit surprises and rapes mortal woman F420.6.1.7.+. (44); wood spirit F441. (46)

SPIRITS appear horrible F401.5. (44); (46); propitiated F406. (50); whistle F262.7.+. (47).–Appearance of spirits F401. (45); means of combating spirits F405. (47); night spirits F470. (44); (47)

SPOILING field with urine K344.2.+. (40)

STAKE.–Head of spirit impaled upon stake S139.2.2.1.+. (44)

STANDS.–Sun stands still F961.1.+. (15)

STAR.–Moon's son is a star A764.1.+. (2)

STARS as children . . . A764.1. (42)

STATUE.–Magic statue kills D1402.19. (9); transformation: statue comes to life D435.1.1. (25)

STILL.–Sun stands still F961.1.+. (15)

STINGINESS. W152. (19); punished Q276. (19)

STOMACH.–How animal gets into person's stomach (or body) . . . B784.1. (22); (23)

STONE.–Woman sinks into stone F943.1.+. (12)

STORM.–Transformation: man to storm D281. (49)

STRANGER.–Task performed by mysterious stranger H976. (5)

STRENGTH.–Culture hero performs . . . feats of strength . . . A526.7. (13)

SUFFER.–Dwarfs suffer abuses . . . F451.5.11. (16)

SUN and his brother rise and set alternately A736.3.3. (2); and moon as brothers A736.3. (2); (42); as cannibal A711.2. (7); (42); does not shine . . . A1010.1. (15); stands still F961.1.+. (15); thrown on fire A1068.+. (2).–Bargain: if the sun resumes its course K194.+. (15); mental powers and disposition of sun A738.2. (42); moon deceives sun A753.3.1. (42)

SUNS.–Originally two suns . . . A711.3.+. (2)

SUPERNATURAL helper . . . N810.4. (10)

SURPRISE.–Night spirit surprises and rapes mortal woman F420.6.1.7.+. (44)

SWALLOWINGS.–Earth swallowings . . . Q552.2.3. (18)

SWAMP.–Drowning in swamp Q467.3.+. (13)

SWINE.–Transformation: man to swine D136. (29)

TABU: fishing during menses C140.+. (22); going forth during menses C141. (42); (44); incest C114. (15); (17); not to touch firestones . . . C145.+. (5); revealing experiences . . . C423.3. (6); sexual intercourse during menses C142. (44); sexual intercourse with unearthly . . . C112. (6).–Flood as punishment for breaking tabu A1018.1. (15)

TAPIR.–Origin of tapir A1889.1.+. (51); transformation: woman to tapir D110.+. (43); (51)

TASK performed by mysterious strangers H976. (5).–Dwarfs help in performing task F451.5.1.20. (16)

TEACH.–Culture hero teaches . . . A541. (41)

TELL.–Animal tells heroine its secret B561.+. (39)

TEST of hero before journey . . . H1250.1. (6)

TESTS of character–misc. H1569. (6)

THREATEN.–Rescued animal threatens rescuer W154.2.1. (34)

THROWN.–Sun thrown on fire A1068.+. (2)

TIGER rescues . . . B545.+. (42)

TIGERS.–Why there is enmity between tigers and man A2585.+. (46)

TINDER.–Origin of flint and tinder A1414.5. (5)

TOUCH.–Tabu: not to touch firestones . . . C145.+. (5)

TRANSFORMATION: animal to clay pipe D429.+. (40); ant to person D382.2. (35); insect to snake D415.+. (35); man to bat D110.+. (37); man to bird D150. (31); man (woman) to monkey D118.2. (49); man to rodent D117. (41); man to storm D281. (49); man to swine D136. (29); man to tree D215. (54); statue comes to life D435.1.1. (25); to child or pet . . . D646.2. (41); to husband's (lover's) form to seduce woman D658.2. (45); tree to person D431.2. (25); trees to field D451.1.+. (43); woman to doe D114.1.1.2. (33); woman to frog D195.+. (2); woman to tapir D110.+. (43); (51); wooden disk to

178

animal D441.+. (32).—Gradual transformation D681. (37); punishment: transformation into frog Q551.3.2.3. (2)

TRANSFORMED.—Parts of human or animal body transformed into plants A2611.0.5. (41)

TRAP.—Tiger rescues man from trap (net) B545.+. (42)

TREACHEROUS host K2294. (11); lord K2247. (16); mistress K2231. (9); relatives-in-law K2218. (24); sister poisons brother K2212.0.1.+. (21); snake K2295.4.+. (34); wife K2213. (43)

TREE as wife T461.3. (25); with extraordinary fruit F811.7. (49).—Abandonment on tree K1113.+. (10); bleeding tree F811.20. (1); marriage with a tree T117.5. (25); residence in tree F562.2. (37); transformation: man to tree D215. (54); transformation: tree to person D431.2. (25)

TREES.—Present habitat of trees . . . A2282.+. (54); transformation: trees to field D451.1.+. (43)

TRIBAL.—New race . . . after tribal calamity A1006.1.+. (15)

TRIBES.—Distribution of tribes A1620. (13)

TROUBLES.—Dwarfs seek human help in their fights and troubles F451.5.23. (8)

TWO.—Originally two suns . . . A711.3.+. (2)

UNBELOVED.—Wife refuses to sleep with unbeloved husband T288. (17)

UNEARTHLY.—Tabu: sexual intercourse with unearthly beings C112. (6)

UNEXPECTED meeting of husband and wife N741. (6)

UNLUCKY accidents N300. (41)

UNUSUAL.—People of unusual diet F561. (8)

UNWITTINGLY.—Lover's flesh eaten unwittingly G61.+. (28)

URINATING.—Husband kills wife by urinating . . . S139.+. (17)

URINE.—Magic urine D1002.1. (41); spoiling field with urine K344.2.+. (40)

VAGINA dentata F547.1.1. (23); husband kills wife by urinating in her vagina S139.+. (17)

VENOMOUS.—Why snakes are venomous A2532.1. (53)

VICTIM enticed . . . K710. (10).—Ogre carries victim in basket G441. (47)

VICTIMS killed while asleep in killer's camp K834.+. (11)

VILLAGES in otherworld F168. (6)

VISIT to land of moon F16. (7); (42)

VIVIFIED.—Mankind from vivified wooden image A1252.1. (1)

VIVIFY.—God makes wooden images and vivifies them A141.1.+. (1)

VOLUNTARY.—Victim enticed into voluntary captivity . . . K710. (10)

VULTURE.—Helpful vulture B455.1. (10)

WALK.—Magic power to walk . . . D2125.1. (10)

WALL around otherworld F148. (6); of water . . . D2151.0.3. (42)

WARD OFF.—Wall of water magically warded off D2151.0.3. (42)

WARN.—Dream warns of danger . . . D1810.8.3.2. (20)

WARNING in dream fulfilled D1810.8.3.1. (20)

WARNINGS.—Inattention to warnings J652. (42); (45)

WARRIORS.—Women warriors or hunters F565. (14)

WATER.—Conception from water T523.+. (10); land of dead across water E481.2. (6); magic power to walk on water D2125.1. (10); wall of water . . . D2151.0.3. (42)

WAY.—Perilous ford on way to otherworld F151.1.4. (6); perilous forest on way to otherworld F151.1.3. (6); spirit with feet turned wrong way F401.9. (46)

WEAPONS.—Origin of white man's weapons A1459.1.+. (10)

WHISTLE.—Spirits whistle F262.7.+. (47)

WHITE.—Origin of white man A1614.9. (10); origin of white man's weapons A1459.1.+. (10)

WIFE banished S411. (28); refuses to sleep with detested husband T288. (17).—Creator's wife A32.3. (1); deserted wife poisons . . . K951.0.1.+. (9); excessive grief at . . . wife's death T211.9. (10); husband eats wife and children G77.+. (11); husband kills wife by urinating . . . S139.+. (17); lazy wife W111.3. (51); treacherous wife K2213. (43); tree as wife T461.3. (25); unexpected meeting of husband and wife N741. (6)

WILD.—Origin of wild boar A1871.1. (52)

WIND.—Revenant as cloud and wind E420.+. (6)

WISDOM (knowledge) acquired from animals J130. (39).—Moon endowed with wisdom and passion A753.3.4. (42)

WOMAN gives birth to snakes T554.7.+. (35); sinks into stone F943.1.+. (12).—Magic journey: woman carried . . . D2121.5.+. (4); night spirit surprises and rapes mortal woman F420.6.1.7.+. (44); punishment: woman eaten . . . Q415.3.+. (19); (22); transformation . . . to seduce woman D658.2. (45); transformation: woman to doe D114.1.1.2. (33); transformation: woman to frog D195.+. (2); transformation: man (woman) to monkey D118.2. (49); transformation: woman to tapir D110.+. (43)

WOMEN warriors or hunters F565. (14)

WOOD.—Creation of man from wood A1252. (1)

WOOD SPIRIT. F441. (46)

WOODEN.—God makes wooden images . . . A141.1.+. (1); mankind from vivified wooden image A1252.1. (1); transformation: wooden disk to animal D441.+. (32)

WOODPECKER.—Helpful woodpecker B461.1. (1)

WORLD.—Entrance to lower world . . . F92.6. (8); return from lower world F101. (6)

WORMS.—Punishment: man eaten by worms (snake) Q415.3. (20); punishment: woman eaten by worms Q415.3.+. (19); (22)

WRONG WAY.—Spirit with feet turned wrong way F401.9. (46)

YAMS.—Origin of yams A2686.4.3. (7)

Glossary

Algarrobo	A tree *(Hymenaea Courbaril)* of the *Leguminosae* family.
Amusha	Brocket deer *(Mazama* sp.).
Arare	The tapir *(Tapirus* sp.).
Arhuakos (Aruakos)	Generic designation for Indian tribes inhabiting the Sierra Nevada de Santa Marta, Colombia, i.e. Kogi, Ica and Sanka, and others cf. Loukotka 1968:242–244.
Arigua	An unidentified species of bees.
Aroka	The silky anteater *(Cyclopes didactylus* ssp.).
Atamara	A bush *(Acalypha diversifolia).*
Atunse	The so-called "axe flute," side-blown, about 110 cm long with four stops in the middle. The air duct, placed at right angles to the air chamber, is fixed in a lump of wax the shape of an axe blade. Unique to the Yupa, the *atunse* is the instrument most befitting their Culture Hero. (For more information regarding the *atunse* see Izikowitz 1935:375; Aretz 1967:224–226.)
Auyama	Collective name for species of *Cucurbita* of subtropical American gourds.
Bacháco	Leaf-cutting ant of the genus *Atta.*
Bagre	Any of various catfishes.
Barama Carib	A Cariban-speaking Indian tribe on the Barama River of Guyana
Barí	A Chibchan-speaking tribe inhabiting the Sierra de Perijá to the south of the Yupa. The Barí are also known as Motilones bravos, Mapé and Kunaguasáya.
Batata	The sweet potato *(Ipomoea batatas).*
Bochaco	An unidentified snake.
Botono	An evil spirit—cause of the common cold.
Cacaruti *(kuruishwu)*	An unidentified tree.
Caimíto	Tree of the genus *Chrysophyllum;* an evergreen tropical American tree also known as star apple. Its purple fruits are edible.

Caña brava	Wild cane. Also referred to as *caña amarga (Gynerium sagittatum)*.
Cashiri	Native beer brewed from a potato or yuca base.
Catío	A Chocoan-speaking Indian tribe on the Cauca River, at the sources of the Sucio River, and on the Murrí and Tugurico Rivers in Colombia.
Ceiba	A massive tree *Ceiba pentandra* bearing large pods filled with seeds invested with a silky floss that yields in the cultivated state the fiber kapok. The *ceiba* is also known as *silk-cotton tree, Bombay ceiba* or *God tree*.
Chamí	A Chocoan-speaking Indian tribe on the Marmato River of Antioquia, Colombia.
Chicha	Native beer made by fermenting various fruits and vegetables.
Churuata	Large communal dwelling of mainly Tropical Forest Indians; *see maloka*.
Coiling	Forming a clay vessel by spiraling wet strands of clay to build up the shape desired.
Conquistador (Sp.)	An original Spanish conqueror. In this context it includes also the German Welser officials.
Coruba	A palm *(Passiflora mollissima)*. Syn. *Curuba*.
Culebra de dos cabezas	A harmless, limbless, lizard *(Amphisbaena fuliginosa)*.
Cuna	A Chibchan-speaking Indian tribe in eastern Panamá.
Guabina	Fishes of the family *Carancínidos*, probably of various genera, which abound in Venezuelan rivers and lakes.
Guamo	Large tree belonging to the family of *Leguminosae* of the *Inga* genus.
Guaymaro	A tree *(Poulsenia armata)* producing edible fruit and a fibrous inner bark very suitable for the production of bark cloth. Syn. *Damagua*.
Gusano cabezón *(makaane)*	The large larvae of an unidentified insect.
Hexagonal weave	In the simplest form, the weaving elements progress in three directions: horizontally, obliquely upward to the right, and obliquely upward to the left.

Homáiki	Ritual song of the Yupa Indians.
Itiriti	A plant *(Ischnosiphon)* with a reed-like stem from which strands for basketry work are prepared.
Jobo	A widely distributed family of trees, *Spondias lutea,* with edible fruits.
Karau	(1) Lord of Animals, (2) evil night spirits.
Kerehi	An unidentified plant.
Kïrïkï	Squirrel *(Sciurus* sp.*)*. Companion of Culture Hero.
Kïrïkmámare	Mother of snakes.
Konochtari	The centipede.
Koronchi	The corroncho *(Chaetostomus guarensis),* a very common freshwater fish.
Kuishna	A hummingbird.
Kusare	See *cashiri.*
Macaurel	A snake *(Corallus hortulanus cookii).*
Makahka	An unidentified wild tuber plant.
Makaane	The large larvae of an unidentified insect, referred to as *gusano cabezón* in the vernacular.
Malanga	Taro *(Colocasia antiquorum).*
Maloka *(maloca,* Sp.*)*	In the present context *maloka* refers to a large communal dwelling of certain Tropical Forest Indian tribes.
Mamón	A tree *(Melicocca bijuga)* of the family *Sapindaceae* producing a fruit surrounded by a delicious sour-sweet pulp.
Manapsa	The name of an Indian tribe which the Yupa, according to their traditional history, displaced when invading the Sierra de Perijá, and which might be identical with the Arahuacos.
Manta	A tunic-like cotton robe worn by men.
Mashíramũ	A bush spirit.
Menure	A large basket with a rectangular base and an elongated elliptical mouth, used for the transportation of field products or water bottles, etc.
Meteru	The name of an Indian tribe which the Yupa,

according to their traditional history, displaced when invading the Sierra de Perijá. They are probably identical with the Barí.

Nonamá

A Chocoan-speaking Indian tribe on the San Juan River in the Chocó territory of Colombia. (Syn. *Chocama, Noanáma, Waunana.*).

Ocumo

A plant *(Xanthosoma sagittifolium)* with large comestible tuberculous roots.

Ojo de zamuro

Mucuna pruriens, a plant belonging to the *Leguminosae.*

Onoto

Red dyestuff prepared from the pulp surrounding the seeds of the onoto (annatto) tree *(Bixa orelleana).*

Opi

A night spirit.

Pamocha

A quid made of tobacco *(Nicotiana tabacum).*

Palma real

The royal palm *(Roystonea regia).* Syn. *Chaguaramo.*

Papaya

A tree *(Carica papaya)* native to tropical America and having large oblong yellow fruit that has a pulpy flesh and thick rind and is eaten raw by the Indians, raw, boiled, pickled or preserved by Creoles.

Páramo

A high bleak plateau or district (as in the Andes), or alpine meadow of northern and western South America.

Pareracha

An unidentified reddish stone.

Pava

Large turkey bird *(Penelope* sp.*)* of the family *Cracidae.*

Peccary

A more or less nocturnal gregarious wild swine (genus *Tayassu*).

Peshewíipi

Lord of all Animals.

Pesowa

A man's straw hat.

Picure

A rodent more commonly known as agouti *(Dasyprocta* sp.*).*

Pigmoid

Term employed here to indicate people resembling by their short stature the Pygmies. No genetic relationship is suggested.

Pipïntu

Dwarf people.

Piri

A gnat.

Pishicáracha	An unidentified bat.
Platano	The plantain or cooking banana *(Musa paradisiaca).*
Porato	The black woolly monkey *(Ateles belzebuth* ssp.)
Sahpatirah plant	*Furcraea* sp.
Sanemá	A northern sub-tribe of the Yanoama Indians of southern Venezuela and northern Brazil.
Sangrito	A tree *(Vismia* sp.) of light wood.
Sapera	An unidentified plant.
Saroro	The otter, nutria *(Pteronura brasiliensis).*
Serémo	A legendary guardian spirit in the form of a giant eagle. He is the Lord of Birds and protects the residence of the Lord of Animals.
Shaman	A person whose power is based on his personal control of supernatural forces.
Shirdi	White-faced monkey *(Cebus albifrons* ssp.)
Tamarind	A widely distributed tropical tree *(Tamarindus indica)* of the family *Leguminosae.*
Tami	Maize flour, non-alcoholic beverage.
Tinamou	Any of numerous birds that constitute the family *Tinamidae.* They resemble gallinaceous birds in habits but are related to the ratite birds.
Tomaira	The Yupa priest-shaman whose shamanic office and realm as a religious practitioner is quite different from that of the *tuano* shaman. The creator of man is said to be the Tomaira Supreme.
Tragavenados	A boa constrictor.
Tuano	Shaman and herbalist. The hispanicized form *tuana* was used to designate the wife of a *tuano.* A *tuana* is also considered to be endowed with supernatural powers.
Tuka	A gruel made of maize *(Zea mays).*
Twill or twilling	Simple weave characterized by diagonal lines formed by the intersection of warp and weft floats. In basketry, twilling produces geometric motifs, frets, and other patterns built up of straight lines.

Uasi	An individual Warao who has achieved a high degree of proficiency as a basket weaver. The Tupinamba paywasu, designating a person who had achieved great fame (Métraux 1948:129), as well as the name for Kanaima's poison employed by various tribes in Guayana (Roth 1915:358–359), may be phonetically and semantically related to the Warao term.
Wahiku	Potter's clay.
Wani	An unidentified snake.
Warao	An Indian tribe inhabiting the swampy lands of the Orinoco Delta in Venezuela.
Wéhra-támí	Fire stones.
Yam	The edible starchy tuberous root of various plants of the genus *Dioscorea.*
Yamore	Legendary Yupa chief.
Yecuana	A Cariban-speaking Indian tribe of southern Venezuela. (Syn. Makiritare.)
Yuca	Sweet yuca *(Manihot dulcis).*
Yuruma	Unidentified plant.

Bibliography

Archivo Nacional de Colombia. *Curas y Obispos,* t.20f.814. Bogotá.

Aretz, Isabel.
1967. *Instrumentos musicales de Venezuela.* Cumaná: Colección La Heredad, Universidad de Oriente.

Bañeres, Jesualdo María de.
1950. *Motilones.* Ediciones Guajiro-Capuchinas, no. 3. Riohacha.

Barnouw, Victor.
1973. *Culture and Personality.* Homewood, Ill.

Benedict, Ruth.
1935. "Zuni Mythology." 2 vols. *Columbia University Contributions to Anthropology,* no. 21. New York.

Benson, Elizabeth P.
1967. *The Maya World.* New York.

Blair, Emma Helen, and James A. Robertson, eds.
1903-1909. *The Philippine Islands 1493-1898.* 55 vols. Cleveland.

Boas, Franz.
1916. "Tsimshian Mythology." Based on Texts Recorded by Henry W. Tate. In *U.S. Bureau of American Ethnology. Thirty-first Annual Report, 1909-1910.* Washington.
1935. "Kwakiutl Culture as Reflected in Mythology." *Memoirs of the American Folklore Society,* v. 28. New York: G.E. Stechert and Company.

Bolinder, Gustaf.
1917. "Einiges über die Motilon-Indianer der Sierra de Perijá (Kolumbien, Südamerika)." *Zeitschrift für Ethnologie,* vol. 49, no. 1:21-51.
1925. *Die Indianer der tropischen Schneegebirge.* Stuttgart.
1958. *We Dared the Andes.* New York.

Bruman, Henry J.
1945. "Early Coconut Culture in Western Mexico." *The Hispanic American Historical Review,* 25(2):212-223.

Chaves, Milciades.
1945. "Mitos, tradiciones y cuentos de los indios Chamí." *Boletín de Arqueología,* 1(2):133-159. Bogotá.

de Booy, Theodor.
1918a. "The Western Maracaibo Lowland, Venezuela." *The Geographical Review,* 6(6):481-500.
1918b. "The People of the Mist: An Account of Explorations in Venezuela." *The Museum Journal,* 9(3-4):183-224. Philadelphia.

Díaz-Ungría, Adelaida G. de, and Helia L. de Castillo.
1971. *Antropología Física de los Indios Irapa.* Caracas: Universidad Central de Venezuela, Facultad de Ciencias Económicas y Sociales, Investigaciones Económicas y Sociales.

Dundes, Alan.
1967. "North American Indian Folklore Studies." *Journal de la Société des Américanistes,* 56(1):53-79. Paris.

Ehrlich, Clara.
1937. "Tribal Culture in Crow Mythology." *Journal of American Folklore*, 40:307–408.

Federmann, Nicolaus.
Indianische Historia. München 1965.

Fernández Yepez, Alberto.
1945. "Anotaciones sobre los indios rionegrinos de Perijá, Venezuela." *Acta Americana*, 3(1,2):64–70.

Fox, Robert B.
1952. "The Pinatubo Negritos: Their Useful Plants and Material Culture." *The Philippine Journal of Science*, 81(3–4):173–414.

Fuchs, Helmut.
1964. "Bibliografía básica de etnología de Venezuela." *Publicaciones del Seminario de Antropología Americana*, vol. 5. Seville: Universidad de Sevilla.

Gabaldon, H.
1941. "Impresiones de un viaje por la inexplorada tierra de Perijá." *Revista Geográfica Americana*, 15:123–130. Buenos Aires.

Gillin, John.
1936. "The Barama River Caribs of British Guiana." *Papers of the Peabody Museum of American Archaeology and Ethnology*, vol. 14, no. 2. Cambridge: Harvard University.

Gusinde, Martin.
1930. "Das Brüderpaar in der südamerikanischen Mythologie." *23rd International Congress of Americanists.* New York.
1956a. "The Yupa Indians in Western Venezuela." *Proceedings of the American Philosophical Society*, 100:198–219. Philadelphia.
1956b. "An Exploratory Study of Indian Pygmies Recently Discovered in the Mountains of Western Venezuela." *Year Book of the American Philosophical Society*, pp. 177–180. Philadelphia.

Hildebrandt, Martha.
1958. "Sistema Fonémico del Macoita: Lenguas Indígenas de Venezuela." Vol. 1. *Publicación de la Comisión Indigenista de Venezuela.* Caracas.

Hitchcock, Charles B.
1954. "The Sierra de Perijá, Venezuela." *Geographical Review*, 54(1):1–28. New York.

Holder, Preston.
1947. "The Motilones: Some Untouched Tropical Forest Peoples in North-Western South America." *Journal of the Washington Academy of Science*, 37(12):417–427. Menasha.

Izikowitz, Karl Gustav.
1935. "Musical and Other Sound Instruments of South American Indians: A Comparative Ethnographical Study." *Göteborgs Kungl. Vetenskaps- och Vitterhets-Samhälles Handlingar.* Göteborg.

Jahn, Alfredo.
1927. *Los aborígenes del occidente de Venezuela.* Caracas.

Koch-Grünberg, Theodor.
1917–1928. *Vom Roroima zum Orinoco: Ergebnisse einer Reise in Nordbrasilien und Venezuela in den Jahren 1911–1913.* 5 vols. Berlin.
Laffer, Luis T.
1959. *Conferencia Pigmoide.* Caracas. MS.
Loukotka, Čestmír.
1968. *Classification of South American Indian Languages.* Latin American Center Publications, Reference Series, vol. 7. Los Angeles: University of California.
Métraux, Alfred.
1948a. "The Tupinamba." Julian H. Steward, ed. *Handbook of South American Indians,* vol. 3, pp. 95–133. Bureau of American Ethnology, Bulletin 143. Washington.
1948b. "Tribes of Eastern Bolivia and the Madeira Headwaters." Julian H. Steward, ed. *Handbook of South American Indians,* vol. 3, pp. 381–454. Bureau of American Ethnology, Bulletin 143. Washington.
Métraux, Alfred, and Paul Kirchoff.
1948. "The Northeastern Extension of the Andean Culture." *Handbook of South American Indians,* 4:349–368. Washington.
Nimuendajú, Curt.
1919–1920. "Bruchstücke aus Religion und Überlieferung der Shipáia-Indianer." *Anthropos,* 14–15:1021–1022. Mödlingen.
Norbeck, Edward.
1950a. "Folklore of the Atayal of Formosa and the Mountain Tribes of Luzon." *Anthropological Papers,* no. 5. Ann Arbor: Museum of Anthropology, University of Michigan.
1950b. "Trans-Pacific Similarities in Folklore: A Research Lead." *Kroeber Anthropological Society Papers,* no. 12, pp. 62–69. Berkeley.
O'Leary, Timothy J.
1963. "Ethnographic Bibliography of South America." *Human Relations Area Files. Behavior Science Bibliographies.* New Haven.
Persson, Lars.
1967. *Motilonernasberg.* Stockholm.
Pineda, Giraldo Robert.
1945. "Los Motilones." *Boletín de Arqueología,* 1(4):349–367. Bogotá.
Reichard, Gladys A.
1947. "An Analysis of Coeur d'Alène Myths." *Memoirs of the American Folklore Society,* vol. 41.
Reichel-Dolmatoff, Gerardo.
1945. "Los indios Motilones: etnografía y lingüística." *Revista del Instituto Etnológico Nacional,* 2(1):15–115. Bogotá.
1953. "Algunos mitos de los indios Chamí (Colombia)." *Revista Colombiana de Folklore,* 2:148–165. Bogotá.
Rochereau, Henri J.
1929. "Nociones sobre las creencias, usos y costumbres de los Catíos del occidente de Antioquia." *Journal de la Société des Américanistes de Paris,* n.s., 21:71–105. Paris.

Roth, Walter E.

1915. "An Inquiry into the Animism and Folk-lore of the Guiana Indians." *Thirtieth Annual Report of the Bureau of American Ethnology (1908-1909)*, pp. 103–386. Washington.

Ruddle, Kenneth.

1970a. *The Yukpa Cultivation System: A Study of Shifting Cultivation and Ancillary Activities in Colombia and Venezuela.* Ph.D. Dissertation. Ann Arbor: University Microfilms.

1970b. "The Hunting Technology of the Maracá Indians." *Antropológica*, 25:21–63. Caracas.

1971. "Notes on the Nomenclature and the Distribution of the Yukpa-Yuco Tribe." *Antropológica*, 30:18–25. Caracas.

1973. "The Human Use of Insects: Examples from the Yukpa." *Biotropica.* Journal of the Association for Tropical Biology, 5 (2):94–101.

1974. *Yukpa Cultivation System: A Study of Shifting Cultivation in Colombia and Venezuela."* Iberoamericana. Berkeley: University of California.

Santelos, Prudencio de.

1959–1960. "Etnografía Yucpa: economía doméstica." *Venezuela Misionera,* 21–22:247–252. Caracas.

Simmons, Donald C.

1961. "Analysis of Cultural Reflection in Efik Folktales." *Journal of American Folklore,* 74:126–141.

Sociedad de Ciencias Naturales La Salle.

1953. *La Región de Perijá y sus habitantes.* Publicaciones de la Universidad del Zulia. Caracas.

Schurz, William Lytle.

1939. *The Manila Galleon.* New York.

Stern, Theodore.

1963. "Ideal and Expected Behavior as Seen in Klamath Mythology." *Journal of American Folklore,* 76:21–30.

Tax, Sol.

1951. *Notes on the Panajachel.* Microfilm Collection of Manuscripts on American Indian Cultural Anthropology, no. 29. Chicago: University of Chicago Library.

Thompson, Stith.

1931–1936. *Motif-Index of Folk Literature.* Indiana University Studies, vols. 19–23. Bloomington.

Vareschi, Volkmar.

1959. *Geschichtslose Ufer.* Wiesbaden.

Vegamian, Félix María de.

1951. "La carretera Machiques-Colón." *Venezuela Misionera,* 13(151):246–248.

Verzosa, Paul R.

1940. *The National Language Ang Pang-bansang Wika.* Manila.

Villamañán, Adolfo de.

1959. "Lenguas e dialectos de los Motilones de Venezuela." *Venezuela Misionera,* 242:74–76; 247:231–233. Caracas.

Vogt, Evon.
1969. *The Zinacantecos of Mexico.* New York.
Wassén, Henry.
1935. "Notes on Southern Groups of Choco Indians in Colombia." *Etnologiska Studier,* 1:35–182. Göteborg.
Wavrin, Robert, Marquis de.
1937. *Moers et coutumes des Indiens sauvages de L'Amérique du Sud.* Paris.
Wilbert, Johannes.
1959. "Puertas del Averno." *Memoria de la Sociedad de Ciencias Naturales La Salle,* 19(54):161–175. Caracas.
1962a. "Zur Kenntnis der Pariri." *Archiv für Völkerkunde,* 15:80–153. Vienna.
1962b. "Erzählgut der Yupa Indianer." *Anthropos,* 57:861–888.
1963. *Indios de la región Orinoco-Ventuari.* Monografía No. 8. Fundación La Salle de Ciencias Naturales. Caracas.
1970. *Folk Literature of the Warao Indians.* Latin American Center Publication, Latin American Studies Series, vol. 15. Los Angeles: University of California.
1972a. *Survivors of Eldorado.* New York.
1972b. "Tobacco and Shamanistic Ecstasy among the Warao Indians of Venezuela." Peter T. Furst, ed., *Flesh of the Gods: The Ritual Use of Hallucinogens.* New York. Pp. 55–83.
1972c. *No Place but the Clouds: Indians of Western Venezuela.* MS.
Wilson, Lawrence L.
1947. *Apayao Life and Legends.* Privately printed, Baguio, Philippines.
Zerries, Otto.
1954. *Wald- und Buschgeister in Südamerika.* Wiesbaden.
1959. "Beiträge zur Anthropologie der Waika- und Shiriana-Indianer im Grenzgebiet zwischen Venezuela und Brasilien." *Zeitschrift für Morphologie und Anthropologie,* 50:31–41. Stuttgart.
Zingg, R.
1934. "American Plants in Philippine Ethnobotany." *Philippine Journal of Science,* vol. 54.